AN UNERRING FIRE

The Massacre at Fort Pillow

RICHARD L. FUCHS

STACKPOLE
BOOKS

Published by
STACKPOLE BOOKS
5067 Ritter Road
Mechanicsburg, PA 17055
www.stackpolebooks.com

Printed in the United States of America

10 9 8 7 6 5 4 3 2 1

FIRST EDITION

Library of Congress Cataloging-in-Publication Data available upon request.

In memory of

William Fuchs
and
Louis Lerner

Contents

List of Illustrations

Preface 2002

Since publication of *An Unerring Fire* in 1994 no new information has been brought to light that would alter the manuscript's thesis: an intentional massacre occurred at Fort Pillow on April 12, 1864. At the time of the original publication many historians did not accept the massacre theory, let alone acknowledge any involvement of the Confederate officers. Two scholars of recent publication, James M. McPherson and Noah Andre Trudeau[1], acknowledge that indeed a massacre occurred. Whether it was an intended act, indulged in by both officers and men of Forrest's forces, still remains shrouded in controversy. Of course there is no doubt in my mind that intentional killing took place and that Forrest was responsible along with other officers of his command. The evidence is as compelling today as it was when *An Unerring Fire* was first published. Only the ghosts of the attacking Confederists would hold to a different conclusion.

The issue of what role, if any, General Forrest played in the affair persists. No evidence has come to light that would dispel the conclusion previously opined by this author that Forrest acquiesced in singling out Federal black troops and their officers as well as Major Bradford and members of his command. General Forrest and his officers did nothing to diffuse what they knew would be the expected outcome should the Confederate forces breach the fort's defenses.

A recent article in a Civil War magazine[2], would attribute the mayhem that occurred that fateful day of April 12, 1864, to a spontaneous reaction that required no specific order. The repugnance the attacking forces felt towards the defenders could not be restrained by inhibitions to wanton killing.

---

[1] James M. McPherson, *For Cause and Comrades: Why Men Fought in the Civil War* (New York: Oxford University Press, 1997); Noah A. Trudeau, *Like Men of War: Black Troops in the Civil War, 1862–1865* (Boston: Little, Brown, 1998).

[2] Mark Grimsley, "Race in the Civil War," *North and South* 4, no. 3 (March 2001): 41.

Again, the demons of sophistry are doing a semantic tape dance to avoid having to fault Forrest for the Fort Pillow atrocities. The killings at Fort Pillow cannot be compared to the spontaneous reactions of a jealous lover, road rage, or an out-of-control family dispute. While many southerners harbored a festering hatred for a perceived inferior race and a paranoiac fear of slaves under arms, the killing at Fort Pillow was not an unforeseen event that merely *happened.* The massacre was intended and anticipated by the attacking command should their men breach the fort's defenses and gain the opportunity. In their minds, the forces of General Forrest had real injustices to avenge that were shared with their commanding officers. A persistent hatred for blacks—and particularly blacks under arms—needing only an opportunity for venting, can hardly be spontaneous.

The facts described herein are persuasive of their own accord. The reader need only keep an open mind.

I am grateful to Stackpole Books for its confidence and support in republishing *An Unerring Fire.*

Preface

The Civil War can be characterized as the most tragic period in American history. Irreconcilable political philosophies and a cultural rivalry borne of deep-seated regional differences combined for years to fan the flames of an uncompromising disdain between the North and South. As the oratory of demagogues increased, the anger and hatred between the sides grew in intensity and the course of war was perforce inevitable. By the year 1861, the country had long passed the point where any hope for a reasonable solution existed. Abraham Lincoln calculated early in his presidency that the total cost of the war, without factoring in the toll of human suffering, would adequately pay for the freedom of every slave. Yet pragmatic considerations such as compensating slave owners and territorial concessions were wholly unrealistic.

After three years of fighting, the animus was not only reflected in the terrible violence on the battlefields, but deeds of unbridled, overt racism prevailed. Racism emerged as a real factor in the war when the North began incorporating former slaves into noncombat military roles. With the formation of volunteer combat units composed of freemen like the 54th Massachusetts the black man's involvement in the war effort became more active. In this regard the Emancipation Proclamation encouraged former slaves from those southern states, which were considered in rebellion against the Federal government, to enlist in the armed services. The swelling ranks of United States Colored Troops (USCT) triggered a corresponding increase in the level of southern outrage and fear.

To be sure, resentment toward blacks was not confined to the Confederate Army. Initially northern prejudice against blacks in the military was quite prevalent among Federal troops and was echoed as well by a government policy that permitted unequal pay and inferior equipment and that assigned blacks to less desirable military duties. Eventually, the successful involvement of black troops in the war effort would ameliorate—to a great extent— their status in the minds of their comrades. The paranoia then existent in the South, however, would never permit a change in attitude toward blacks without Confederates first acting out on the battlefield their fear of blackmen under arms.

Perhaps, nowhere in all of the theaters of operation, was the fury of this hatred to find meaner and more violent expression than along the Tennessee banks of the Mississippi River at Fort Pillow. The tragedy that occurred there had no precedence elsewhere in the Civil War. All of the bitterness that existed between the contending forces was exacerbated by the presence of blacks under arms who fought alongside white Tennesseans who had chosen the uniform of the Union Army rather than enlisting in the Confederate cause. The engagement lasted about nine hours, but the events that occurred after the fort's last defenses were breached created a controversy that, to this day, remains shrouded in conflict. Specifically, the dispute revolves around two key issues: first, whether or not the heavy losses suffered by the Federal garrison occurred as a result of their own incompetence or the normal vagaries of war; and, second, whether or not a deliberate massacre occurred that was the intended objective of the Confederate commanding general, Nathan Bedford Forrest, and his subalterns.

Several Forrest biographies exonerate him from any criminal culpability, maintaining the excessive casualties were wholly the fault of the garrison. Other contemporary authors, while acknowledging the killing was wanton disregard for human life, maintain that the proof is, at best, ambiguous and uncertain regarding the general's involvement. This book has attempted to digest the official records, reports, documents, and eyewitness statements with an analysis of the respective arguments presented by either Forrest supporters or Confederists. To accomplish this objective, Forrest's early life and personality, the political climate, related events, the underlying circumstances of the engagement, public reaction, and the effect the incident had in the Union Army were considered. The result has been a finding that a deliberate massacre occurred. General Forrest participated in the affair through either a deliberate failure to control his forces or by subtly encouraging a result he sought and knew would be the inevitable consequence of a Confederate victory over the garrison. That an intentional massacre occurred at the instigation or with the tacit approval of General Forrest and his command is clearly and convincingly established by the record.

The primary sources for ascertaining the Confederist point of view have been the works of the principal Forrest biographers,

Ralph Seph Henry, Dr. John A. Wyeth, and General Thomas Jordan and John P. Pryor. The rationales explored by contemporary scholars Shelby Foote, John Cimprich, Robert C. Mainfort Jr., Albert Castel, Jack Hurst, and Brian Wills were also utilized. Not surprisingly the biographers have cloaked Forrest with all the hues of a colorful folk hero. Much of their analysis of the Fort Pillow incident and General Forrest's involvement appears steeped in regional pride and historical preferences as well as a less than dispassionate adoration for General Forrest. This absence of objectivity is obvious from some disingenuous arguments of the no massacre theorists. When Dr. Wyeth, an early Forrest biographer, suggests, for example, that the black man's penchant for alcohol contributed to the garrison's failed defenses and caused the reckless behavior demonstrated by the defenders after the fort was stormed, the very prejudices that inspired the massacre become the basis for purported scholarly analysis. As the facts will demonstrate, even the basis for asserting the garrison consumed alcohol during the engagement is highly suspect and impeachable. Other writers have circuitously argued that no massacre occurred because General Sherman would have ordered reprisals if the proof existed. As demonstrated by this work, proof of the massacre was evident, but Sherman intentionally declined to order reprisals and opted for a more natural recourse.

The improbabilities, suppositions, and rationalizations inherent in pro-Forrest arguments appear more designed to prevent any distraction from the hero worship that follows Forrest in death as it enveloped him during his life. Each side in the controversy, it is true, has attempted through subtleties in presentation, restricted and selected evaluation of evidence, and hyperbole to promote their arguments. In sifting through the relevant evidence in a historical context, the truth of what happened at Fort Pillow on 12 and 13 April 1864 leaves little doubt. Like lawyers before a jury during summation, historians may juggle the facts, but the common experiences of veniremen are enough to ascertain the true state of events.

At the commencement of this project I had no particular preference regarding the Fort Pillow dispute. Some cursory reading of the incident peaked my curiosity, which was then nurtured through the pursuit of additional information. Being an historian by avocation, I decided to explore the subject purely for the satisfaction of learning as an end in itself. Within the array of points and counterpoints proposed by the several noted scholars, I was confident "real" truth, not the "somewhere in between" truth could be found. However, not until I sifted through original source material did a clearer picture emerge.

I soon discovered that satisfying my personal quest would not suffice. The engagement at Fort Pillow does not approach the enormous physical conflicts characteristic of the more popular Civil War battles in which tens of thousands were pitted against each other in desperate struggles for survival. The incident at Fort Pillow, however, with its own tragic occurrences and unconscionable indifference to human life presents a compelling story that needed to be accurately told. The purpose of *An Unerring Fire* is to examine a moment in one of the great dramas in American history, to put aside the detached romanticism of some historians, and to capture the cold chilling truth of the event with the hope of bringing closure to the controversy and honor to the memory of those who suffered.

In reaching the conclusions contained here, I was initially perplexed by a question of philosophical significance. In judging Nathan Bedford Forrest and his forces, are we to be guided by the attitudes of Southern society in antebellum America, or are our present values respecting right and wrong conduct to govern? True, Nathan Bedford Forrest's attitude toward blacks reflected the acceptable cultural and political sentiments of his time and locale. An awareness of this attitude only gives explanation but does not justify that conduct. Neither does the acclaim of a folk hero alter the fact or make deminimis Forrest was a racist in a racist society. Although events can often be explained in a historical framework, abhorrent behavior is not as dependent upon the time of retrospection as much as it is a reflection of what is right or wrong for all seasons. Slavery, for example, is an odious institution irrespective of the time or place of evaluation and however contrived the rationalization. In this regard a different time or place can not justify the slaughter of any people. Unfortunately, when we excuse the kind of mayhem that occurred at Fort Pillow because it was a catharsis of feelings indigenous to the times and generated by the prevalent perceptions of nineteenth-century America, we give approval to incidents of barbarity at the expense of our own humanity. The deaths and injuries at Fort Pillow occurred because the object of the attack was not the fort itself but the forces aligned behind the breastworks. The affair at Fort Pillow was simply an orgy of death, a mass lynching to satisfy the basest of conduct—intentional murder—for the vilest of reasons—racism and personal enmity.

Acknowledgments

I seriously doubt that any author can boast a manuscript that is solely the product of his or her efforts. This publication experience is my first venture into the world of Gutenberg. If I have come away with one lasting impression, it is that one's success is dependent upon a variety of influencing minds and caring souls. As is usually the case in major projects of this nature, without the compassionate encouragement and unselfish expertise of others I might still be groping for closure. These confidantes of new origin as well as old acquaintances have nurtured the author through many a crisis of seemingly insurmountable confusion. Of course, the moment the publisher's letter of acceptance is received all the hours of frustration, the lengthy pursuits for connecting phrases, the tedium of dangling thoughts, the nightmare searches for lost citations, and whatever else is the bane of authorship pass into an obscurity of faint images.

What does remain, like the lingering fragrance of myrrh and frankincense, are the many recollections of those who gave direction; those who shared their knowledge, shortcut the chase for information, or otherwise gave aid and comfort to the author. While I am indebted to many, several deserve special recognition: the staffs of the main branch at the Memphis Shelby County Library and Information Center, the main branch of the New York Public Library, the Warner Library in Tarrytown, New York, and the U.S. Military Academy Library at West Point. I extend special thanks to Patricia M. LaPointe for her assistance and interest in my work and to the members of the reference and Adult Services section at the Warner Library for their many courtesies and time-saving help. I was delighted to have made the acquaintance of Alan C. Aimone, chief, Special Collections, U.S. Military Academy Library. Aimone provided me with invaluable insights into the research and autopiloted me through the right stacks. His Civil War expertise and awareness of conceivably every military manuscript in the academy's impressive library is, to say the least, awesome.

Grateful appreciation is extended to the Division of Archaeology, Tennessee Department of Environment and Conservation, Memphis; the Photo Duplication Service, Library of Congress, Washington, D.C.; the Anne S. K. Brown Military Collection, Brown University Library, Providence, Rhode Island; the United States Military History Institute, Department of the Army, Carlisle, Pennsylvania; The Library of America, New York; the Civil War Times Illustrated, Harrisburg, Pennsylvania; and William Konecky Associates, New York, for their cooperation and courtesy in permitting me to reprint or adapt the photographs, maps, illustrations, and quotations that appear in this manuscript. Special gratitude is extended to Keith Axelrod, president, and Herb Lamb of Action Advertising, Fishkill, New York, for generously providing me with their artistic talent and valuable time in producing the Fort Pillow Battle Site illustration and the adaptation of the geographical map.

My visit to the Fort Pillow State Historic Area was the most pleasant and rewarding event in putting together *An Unerring Fire*. Ranger Roy Harkness and his lovely wife, Margaret, extended to me all the gracious hospitality for which we northerners hear the South is famous. I spent an entire day exploring every facet of the fort's restoration, observing aspects not likely to be seen by the ordinary visitor. Roy shared with me his private papers and his depth of knowledge. He may not agree with several aspects of this book's thesis, but I am confident the bonds of friendship sewn that day will long survive any disputes we may have concerning the Fort Pillow massacre.

Since the best may be savored last, there is my wife Fredda—a very special human being who is my friend and confidante. She indulged me this project with a disposition that was at times controlled but always loving and supportive. More than anyone she is glad the manuscript has reached the finality of publication. No longer will the recreation room be strewn with papers or will hours of my time be consumed hunting for an obscure fact. Indeed conversations can resume the mutuality of normal discourse. While I am grateful for the loving partnership, Fredda's encouragement, intelligent observations, and inquiries were of immeasurable assistance.

I am also mindful of the influence of Judge Simon Sobeloff, chief justice for the Fourth Circuit Court of Appeals, and Professor Herbert Gutman. Cousin Sobeloff insisted I study history if I wanted to pursue a career in the law. Professor Gutman made the study of history a remarkable experience and introduced me to my first encounter with the American Civil War— an encounter that has become an unquenchable search for knowledge and truth.

An Unerring Fire

Introduction

It was 12 April 1864. North of Memphis, Tennessee the flood-
waters of the Mississippi River were receding since the spring
thaw had arrived early that year. The seasonal time clock was
awakening regional plants as warmer air and moist soil nurtured
new life. Across the landscape could be seen the faint hint of green
as sweet gum, hickory, oak, cottonwood, and other indigenous
hardwood trees stirred. Sweet William and wild dogwood added
their hues. Three years earlier on this date the Civil War began
with the firing on Fort Sumter. The Battle of Shiloh had been
fought in April two years earlier, and the campaign to capture
Vicksburg began the same month the previous year.

With the fall of Vicksburg and Port Hudson along the Mississippi River in 1863, Abraham Lincoln expressed the optimism,
perhaps prematurely, that the "Father of Waters" again went "un-
vexed to the sea." In the east, the Army of the Potomac under
General George Meade in July 1863 defeated General Robert E.
Lee at Gettysburg, reversing with finality the southern strategy to
carry the war to the North. Other major battles had whittled away
Confederate resources and reduced their territorial integrity. In
April 1864, General William Tecumseh Sherman was preparing
his infamous march through Georgia and on to the sea. Also
during that month General Ulysses S. Grant was preparing to
move east where, as commander of all Federal troops, he would
lead the Army of the Potomac during the next agonizing year to
final victory in April 1865.

These were difficult times for a war-weary nation. The number
of dead and wounded suffered by both sides in major battles
and engagements as of 9 April 1864 approximated 317,538.[1] The
casualties arising from the conflict created an alarming drain
upon resources in the country. In the south the "seceshs" had to
have felt the excesses of war more than their northern adversaries.
In the state of Tennessee and elsewhere along the Mississippi
frontier the country bore witness to farmlands and plantations
ravaged by foraging troops. Cities were devastated, homes and
agricultural enterprises destroyed, and anything thought useful

to the enemy was burned. The destruction of means of travel and communication, and the hordes of starving refugees and meandering former slaves were a common sight. The ferociousness of the battles and major engagements had no parallel in American history and would reach unprecedented numbers by the end of the war.[2]

Whatever may have been the gallant hopes of its brave officers and men, in 1864 the Confederate Army must have sensed, albeit privately, the impending doom. Notwithstanding their willingness to continue the fray, men like General Nathan Bedford Forrest were well aware of what was happening to the land, its people, and their property. The Federal land victories, together with the tightening naval blockade, augured anything but a realistic hope of victory for the Confederacy. Indeed, seven years after Appomattox, General Forrest acknowledged that as early as eighteen months before the war's end he was convinced the South was defeated.[3] Confederate battlefield successes were only momentary celebrations without any appreciable impact upon the war's outcome. The strategies planned would do little more than delay, not deter, the Union juggernaut.

By April 1864, the country had long passed the point where the conflagration of national disunity was even close to a semblance of civility. In fact, the scorched earth policy inherent in war was to reach new heights by one of the great architects of "war is hell." The preceding year the Federal government issued instructions to its armies in the field observing that

> military necessity admits of all direct destruction of life or limb or armed enemies, and of other persons whose destruction is incidentally unavoidable in the armed contests of the war; it allows of the capturing of every armed enemy, and of every enemy of importance to the hostile government, or of peculiar danger to the captor; it allows of all destruction of property and obstructions of the ways and channels of traffic, travel, or communication and of all withholding of sustenance or means of life from the enemy; of the appropriation of whatever an enemy's country affords necessary for the subsistence and safety of the army.

These General Orders, dated April 1863, also expressed the expectation that the same men who took "up arms against one another in public war do not cease on this account to be moral beings, responsible to one another and to God."[4] Tragically, by April 1864 the morals of the battlefield were inextricably tied to more primitive instincts.

On 12 April 1864, then Major General Nathan Bedford Forrest, in command of the Confederate Cavalry Department of West Tennessee and North Mississippi, led a force of over eighteen hundred "mounted infantry" against a federal garrison at Fort Pillow consisting of from 578 to 585 officers and men. Fort Pillow was situated on a bluff some thirty-five to forty miles north of Memphis, Tennessee, along the east bank of the Mississippi River, across from Arkansas. Before noon of the next day 61 percent of the total forces defending the fort would be counted among the dead and wounded, with about 43 percent, or 248, killed. Of the survivors, 226 were either not wounded or not so disabled as to prevent their removal by General Forrest as prisoners. The remaining garrison of approximately 110 men were either paroled or, after hiding along the banks of the river, made their way to the safety of federal troops, who arrived during the following two days on river vessels.[5] In this group, the majority were seriously wounded, and thirty-one would not survive.

Some historians regard the 43 percent loss of life as "no means an extraordinary high rate for a place carried by assault."[6] Indeed, if these figures alone were determinative, the incident at Fort Pillow would have been lost in history as another minor, obscure Civil War engagement. The incident was hardly insignificant. The Fort Pillow casualty ratio of two and one-half dead for each wounded Union soldier is far in excess of the generally accepted ratio of Civil War casualties of one dead for each six to eight wounded in battle.[7] When comparing these casualty figures with the relatively slight losses sustained by General Forrest's troops, fourteen killed and eighty-six wounded,[8] and in light of the garrison's racial and geopolitical composition, one can scarcely argue that unnecessary and deliberate killing had not occurred. More precisely, the percentage losses between black and white Federal troops, as well as the high incidence of dead and wounded in a skirmish of this nature, lends credence to a more sinister conclusion: an intentional design to annihilate the garrison for reasons unrelated to strategic objectives or military necessity.

Although casualty figures are not wholly reliable and vary among historians and the official records, it is reasonable to conclude that among the defenders of the fort approximately 170 blacks and about 80 whites were killed during the first twenty-four hours, with total mortalities exceeding 280. This then represents a kill ratio of 66 percent among the blacks and 35 percent among the white federal troops.[9] Of the 226 prisoners taken by Forrest's forces, only 58 were black, whereas 168 were white.[10]

General Forrest's biographers (such as Dr. John A. Wyeth, who served with veterans of Forrest's original command during the last two years of the war) would arrive "at a conclusion unbiased by prejudice," that there was no massacre.[11] One modern Confederist could make a distinction between the word slaughter as used to commonly describe the aftermath of battle and the word massacre as it applies to the battle at Fort Pillow. This biographer grudgingly concedes the happening of a massacre "seems" to have occurred at Fort Pillow because the federal troops were shot down in large numbers when they no longer could offer resistance. Other historians concede that at worst "unnecessary killing had occurred,"[12] but General Forrest's involvement cannot be proven. Taking into account the totality of circumstances and leadership influencing the attacking forces and giving rise to the attack itself, and estimating even more conservative casualty figures, one is compelled to conclude that there is "unmistakable evidence of a massacre carried on long after any resistance could have been offered, with cold-blooded barbarity and perseverance which nothing can palliate,"[13] which had its origins in racism and political antagonism. The numerous and specific nature of the injuries suffered by the survivors and their vivid recollections paint a convincing and horrid picture. Eyewitness statements from military personnel and correspondents arriving the following morning tend to confirm these excesses.

The controversy that has survived to this day is not limited to whether a massacre occurred. The debate focuses as well upon General Forrest's participation. Much of the evidence relative to the happening of the occurrence is equally probative of General Forrest's involvement. Sufficient proof exists to justify a finding that the massacre was a natural and intended consequence of General Forrest and his troop's personal enmity toward this particular garrison. An analysis of official military correspondence and other documentary proof reveal a number of relevant events bearing upon this issue. The citizenry of the countryside had compiled a list of serious offenses committed upon them by Major Bradford's 13th Tennessee Cavalry or other Federal commanders. There was substantial proof that the garrison was composed of a number of Confederate deserters from Forrest's own command. Clearly, there were personal vendettas to be avenged and an urgency to right past grievances. Two previously unreported incidents involving the confession of a Confederate spy and the statement of a Confederate conscript give convincing evidence that a design to teach the garrison a few lessons was anticipated by those associated with General Forrest's command.

Throughout the war, General Nathan Bedford Forrest's distinguished military successes gained for him a reputation for fearlessness, daring, and aplomb on the battlefield. These same traits marked his civilian life as well, where his decisions were made with unshakable resolve and executed with summary dispatch. His initial years were a precursor of what his military career was to become. The forces that shaped Nathan Bedford Forrest's early life made inevitable the type of disaster that occurred 12 April 1864. It was only a matter of time. The Civil War provided the arena and Fort Pillow the place.

1

The Devil Forrest

On 13 July 1821 in a frontier cabin of impoverished surroundings, Miriam Beck Forrest gave birth to fraternal twins: Nathan Bedford Forrest and his sister, Fannie. The area was known as Chapel Hill, middle Tennessee, in a county then called Bedford. The Forrests were to have five more sons and two daughters. William Forrest, father of Nathan, could trace his ancestry in the United States to 1730. He was a blacksmith by trade and he possessed all the restlessness of a spirited pioneer.

At the time Nathan was thirteen years of age, the Forrests collected the essentials of a spartan, frontier existence and moved to Tippah County in northern Mississippi where they homesteaded on lands recently vacated by the Chickasaw Indians. The area was sparsely populated, and the nearest hamlet, Salem, was a distance away. William died in 1837, and Nathan, not yet sixteen years old had to shoulder the heavy responsibility as head of the household. His burdens as titular head became more complicated when, four months after his father's death, Nathan's younger brother, Jeffrey, was born. Nathan raised Jeffrey as if he was his own son. Miriam Beck married six years later, giving birth to three more sons and a daughter.

The Forrests' life in Tippah county was marked by "poverty, toil and responsibility."[1] From sunrise to sunset Nathan would tend the fields. At night he would continue his labors by candlelight as he made buckskin clothing and footwear for his siblings. Here he acquired the traits of self-reliance and fortitude while cherishing the nonconformity and individualism a frontier environment nurtured. The demands of forced adulthood and frontier isolation afforded him only six months of schooling, which was all the formal education he was to have during his life. The harshness of rural and remote surroundings would also take its toll on the health of Nathan's three sisters who succumbed to early deaths.

At the age of twenty, Nathan left home and joined a volunteer military company to fight for Texas in what was then rumored to be an imminent threat of invasion by Mexico. War with Mexico did not occur until 1846, and during Nathan's early military experience, he was to receive substantially less tutoring than his several months of schooling.

Upon returning home in 1842 he joined his uncle, Jonathan Forrest, in the latter's livestock and livery stable business then located in Hernando, Mississippi. With his other brothers of sufficient maturity and stature to care for their mother's farm, Nathan undoubtedly saw this partnership with his uncle as an opportunity to escape the shackles of poverty and privation. The partnership lasted until 1845 when the elder Forrest, in not uncharacteristic fashion for those lawless frontier times, was shot down and killed in the street as a result of a personal feud. Nathan Bedford Forrest married in the same year and continued to reside in Hernando until 1851. In that year the demands of his expanding business interests necessitated that his wife, son, and daughter move to Memphis, Tennessee, twenty miles north. There he pursued numerous interests relating to the burgeoning and increasingly popular economy of cotton. He dealt in real estate, eventually owning two tracts of land, one of which was a plantation of three thousand acres. He successfully grew and marketed cotton on lower Mississippi lands that were particularly adaptable for this demanding crop. His livestock business was augmented by the lucrative trade of slaves.

While in Memphis he ran for public office and held the position of alderman until the outbreak of the Civil War. In 1859 he closed the real estate and slave businesses in order to devote his time entirely to his plantation interests. By 1861, with a production of one thousand bales of cotton and an annual income of $30,000.00, he had amassed, by his own estimate, $1.5 million before the war.[2] While his slave trading enterprise did not obtain for him the social status of those plantation gentry who purchased his human wares, and he was not able to shed the cloak of a back woodsman's mores for the social graces of a Southern aristocrat,[3] he was a personage of noted reputation in the community and "a man of substance and standing in the commercial world."[4]

When Tennessee finally voted to secede from the Union in June 1861, Nathan Forrest enlisted as a private in Company D of a regiment that was to become legendary as the Seventh Tennessee Cavalry. He did not stay long with this outfit, but using his own resources recruited a battalion of Mounted Rangers. His reliance upon his own funds for equipping and supplying his forces and the impact the conflict had upon the southern economy nearly bankrupted him by war's end. "I came out of the war pretty well wrecked . . . completely used up, shot all to pieces, crippled up . . . a beggar."[5]

Nathan Forrest was not the only member of the family to do service for the Confederate cause. His youngest brother, Jeffrey, a brigadier general, was killed at the age of twenty-six leading a charge against General Sturgis's rear guard at Okolona, Mississippi. The fourth son, Aaron, was a lieutenant colonel, who died of pneumonia during the expedition to Paducah, Kentucky, in 1864. A captain of scouts, William Forrest was wounded several times; in April 1863, he had his leg shattered by a Minie ball while leading a charge against Colonel Abel Streight's forces at the foot of Sand Mountain in northern Alabama.

Captain William Forrest had the reputation, not unlike his older brothers, Nathan and John, of being "modest and reticent in his demeanor, yet possessed that quality of courage which did not seem to realize what fear meant. He was quick to resent an insult, and following the rule that prevailed in the frontier community . . ., he believed the only way to settle a dispute was to fight it out."[6]

The second oldest brother, John, could not enlist in the Confederate Army; he had been partially paralyzed by a bullet received during the Mexican War. He would nevertheless make a contribution to the southern war effort. Residing in Memphis, where in 1862 the city was garrisoned by Federal troops, his mother came to him to complain about the insulting behavior of a Union officer while passing through their homestead. When the officer happened by the hotel where John lived, heated remarks were exchanged between the two. John rose on one crutch and attempted to strike the officer with the other. The officer kicked the supporting crutch out from underneath John who toppled to the ground. While prostrate, John drew a derringer and inflicted near fatal wounds to the officer. Following his arrest and trial John was acquitted of any wrongdoing.

Of Nathan Forrest's half brothers, "two of the younger Luxton sons of Miriam Beck—boys still in their teens—became soldiers in the Confederate service while, at the very last, the third and youngest of the Luxton boys, not yet sixteen left his mother's farm and passed through the lines to join the failing forces of the Confederacy."[7]

Nathan Bedford Forrest was tall, six foot two inches, with a powerful build of athletic proportions. His deep gray-blue eyes set in high cheeks, beard and wavy hair, gave him an imposing look of "striking and commanding presence"[8] and an appearance of stern seriousness. This "dour and harsh figure"[9] never smoked or used vulgar language although he was disposed to a mean and violent temper. He is claimed to have drunk liquor only when wounded and that his only vice was gambling. His associates described him as "extremely neat" and "scrupulously clean."

He had a naturally soft voice and expressed gentle tenderness toward children, his wife, his mother, and women generally and was reportedly humane to his slaves. During his entire life, he exhibited a pious, religious reverence that found expression in evoking God's blessing at the beginning of every expedition. He reportedly did not take kindly to any members of his command who exhibited disrespect during these prayer assemblies. On one occasion he summoned a captured Union chaplain to his mess to pronounce the blessing before dinner and then released him to care for the sinners on the other side.[10]

This soft, genteel exterior was contrasted with a desperate and destructive nature, a maelstrom of discontent. An "unusual combination of piety and reckless violence"; a "mixed nature, compounded of violence and of gentleness"; "arbitrary, imperious and determined"; "fierce and terrible"; and a "harsh and violent temper"[11] are commonly accepted descriptions of his dichotomous personality.

Forrest the slave trader was described as having been kind to his human wares. From his slave market in Memphis he would permit his slaves the liberty to go out about the city and surrounding environs for the purpose of choosing their own master. There was never any instance of a slave running away because while he taught them to abide the privilege "he also taught them to fear him exceedingly."[12]

Forrest was gentle as long as one did not cross him. He was tender to those who posed no threat. Having assumed the posture of an adult at the age of sixteen, a difficult time and place for a young man to lose his father, his life was very much a struggle. He fought not only to survive the harshness of a backwoods existence but to break the bonds of an impoverished life-style and to look after and protect all those who were dependent upon him for their survival, as well. He was the unquestionable authority over the affairs of his family, business interests, and life. With a jealous zeal and an unbounded and unabashed energy, he tenaciously protected that which was his, against any outside threat, real or imagined.

General Nathan Bedford Forrest. Courtesy of the Library of Congress.

Forrest's idiosyncratic personality was characterized by a certain Jekyll-and-Hyde quality. His alternating between moods of soft tenderness and bellicose aggression was no enigma. Clearly, his behavior was the product of a harsh, demanding, and rugged early life. Because of a life-style that was not without its disappointments and inherent cruelty, he had to provide his own role model. Notwithstanding the affection he had for his mother, her stern and disciplinary ways (for she was not one to spare the rod) had its measurable impact. While it is ludicrous to suggest his rebelliousness and resentment were the result of a "sinister preference" for being left-handed,[13] Forrest's inner anger and violent disposition was influenced by the reality of his environment and the burdens of his responsibilities. There was to be no compromise with either his self-reliance or nonconformity. Challenges that threatened the fruits of his industry and hard work could not go unanswered. To do otherwise would mean to compromise and threaten his very existence and the existence of those who were dependent upon him.

Nathan Bedford Forrest was a primed cannon that would rather explode in devasting impact upon his adversary than to adjust any dispute through reason. Forrest's gentle demeanor masked an inner dimension of anger that revealed itself as a vicious propensity to do great violence.

When Forrest was about nineteen, his mother and her sister were returning from a visit to a distant neighbor. As dusk began to envelop their horseback ride home, a catamount caught the scent of chickens Miriam Beck was carrying in a basket. As they galloped closer to home, the cougar, in overtaking the pair, lunged onto the back of Miriam Beck while at the same time clawing the horse's back. In fright, the horse plunged forward causing the panther to lose its grip. As the panther fell, it tore at Miriam Beck's clothing inflicting severe wounds about her shoulders.

After she was carried into the cabin, Forrest got his dogs and rifle, and despite the protestations of his mother and the lateness of the hour, started out to track the animal. Determined to kill the animal, he followed his dogs all night until he treed the cougar. Then, waiting for daylight, he "sent a bullet through its heart." Still not satisfied, he cut off the scalp and ears of the catamount to present as a trophy to his mother.

At another time, after giving due warning to a neighbor as to the consequences should the farmer's ox again trample the fences and crops about the Forrest homestead, Nathan, as he had promised, shot and killed the ox when the animal again strayed into their cornfield. When the farmer came to investigate the commotion with rifle in hand, Forrest leveled his cocked flintlock at the farmer warning him if he made any untoward action, Forrest would kill him. The farmer withdrew.

In 1845, a dispute arose between his uncle Jonathan and four local planters. Forrest told the group he was not involved in the dispute but could not stand by and allow his uncle to be unfairly assailed and mistreated. Forrest had barely finished speaking when one of the ruffians drew a pistol and fired at him. The shot grazed Forrest and caused a general exchange of fire. The older Forrest was mortally wounded.[14] Though slightly wounded himself, Forrest drew a double-barrel pistol and shot two of his assailants, killing one and wounding another. He grabbed a bowie knife from a bystander and chased the other two from the town.

General Forrest was wounded several times during the war. On one occasion, a disgruntled artillery officer nearly succeeded in killing him. Disappointment regarding the young officer's transfer prompted him to confront Forrest, and, after a heated exchange, he shot the general above the left hip. Forrest held the officer's pistol grip with one hand, and securing a penknife between his teeth, opened the knife with his free hand and plunged the blade into the officer's abdomen. The officer fled, and when Forrest learned his own wound might be fatal, he promised "No damned man shall kill me and live." He grabbed a pistol from the saddle of a hitched horse and pursued his assailant. The altercation was terminated only after Forrest was persuaded by others that the officer was dying.[15]

It is not the justification or self-defense that is striking in these incidents. Rather, it is the utter commitment to the complete annihilation of his adversaries—the uncontrolled torrent of rage that could not be satiated short of total destruction of the threat. During the Battle of Chickamauga the Confederates had succeeded in routing all but General Thomas's troops who held firm to a position with rallied stragglers while under attack from three sides. General Rosecrans was able to successfully withdraw his army to the safety of the Chattanooga because the Confederates did not mount a coordinated pursuit. General Forrest implored the Confederate Commander, General Bragg to "press forward as rapidly as possible" and insisted that "every hour is worth ten thousand men"[16] without effect. For his efforts he was ordered to turn over his command to General Wheeler of the cavalry, to whom on a previous occasion Forrest swore "I'll be in my coffin before I'll fight again under your command." General Forrest rode to Bragg's headquarters's tent where he verbally abused and threatened his commander.

After denouncing General Bragg as a coward and liar, and rebuking him for taking away his brigade, Forrest concluded:

> I have stood your meanness as long as I intend to. You have played the part of a damned scoundrel, and are a coward, and if you were any part of a man I would slap your jaws and force you to resent it. You may as well not issue any more orders to me, for I will not obey them, and I will hold you personally responsible for any further indignities you endeavor to inflict upon me. You have threatened to arrest me for not obeying your orders promptly. I dare you to do it, and I say to you that if you ever again try to interfere with me or cross my path it will be at the peril of your life."[17]

During this "shower of invective" General Bragg undoubtedly knew Forrest was not accountable to law or reason, and the slightest objectionable reaction could have proved fatal. Bragg sat quietly.

General Forrest's wrath was not reserved for superior officers. At Murfreesboro he shot his color bearer during the engagement; at Brentwood he did the same to another panic stricken Confederate; and at West Point, Forrest leaped from his horse and gave a soldier the "worst thrashing" his subordinate, General Chalmers, had ever seen.[18] Dr. Wyeth, his biographer, justifies these actions, for in Forrest's "mind the killing of one of his own soldiers now and then as an example of what a coward might expect, was a proper means to the end."[19]

During "paroxyms of excitement" Forrest displayed a "noticeable physical peculiarity." "His complexion, which was naturally sallow, changed completely in color. The capillaries became so greatly engorged with blood that the skin of the face and neck took on almost a scarlet hue. The blood vessels of the eye took on the same congestion, giving him an expression of savageness that could not be misunderstood. Everything that was suggestive of kindly feeling or tenderness seemed to vanish from his nature as thoroughly as if his heart had never throbbed with human sympathy. His voice, naturally soft, became harsh, husky, and metallic in tone."[20]

At Murfreesboro in July 1862, after successfully surprising and finally capturing General Crittenden's forces who were garrisoned there, Forrest's men rescued Confederate prisoners from a jail that a Union trooper deliberately set afire. One of the prisoners recalling the event years later described Forrest's appearance on that occasion: "eyes were flashing as if on fire, his face was deeply flushed, and he seemed in a condition of great excitement." This survivor then related what followed.

> After the fighting had ceased and the federal prisoners were all brought together, General Forrest came to me and said: "They tell me these men treated you inhumanly while in jail. Point them out to me." I told him there was but one man I wished to call his attention to, and that was the one who had set fire to the jail in order to burn us up. Forrest asked me to go along the line with him and point that man out. I did so. A few hours later, when the list of the private soldiers were being called, the name of this man was heard and no one answered; Forrest said, "Pass on, it's all right."[21]

Following the biblical axiom for retribution and applying a frontiersman's sense of summary justice, Forrest undoubtedly had the Federal trooper executed. It was not to be the last time his rage would govern his actions.

General Forrest observed that "war means fighting and fighting means killing." He postured that if he could get there first with the most men he could win.[22]

Contrary to the beliefs of his opponents both on and off the battlefield, this confession of strategy was often not the case, and his success was more aptly the result of unique and unorthodox tactics and the ruse of making it appear he had more troops than were actually on the field. This uneducated backwoodsman, of untutored military genius, evolved a strategy that became his hallmark. Feigning an attack at the center of the enemy's lines, he secreted forces to the flank and rear. When his forces moved in from the sides, Forrest would wait for confusion to arise within the enemy's ranks, and then charge with reckless abandon into the whole of the enemy's front. He deployed his cavalry as infantry. After dismounting and forming skirmish lines, his troops were encouraged to use whatever cover the field of engagement afforded.

General Forrest was clearly a military leader of unparalleled courage and daring who would never hesitate to do battle. Except when large numbers of troops had to be deployed, he was more comfortable and eager to be in the middle of the fray. During his career as a Confederate cavalry commander he had twenty-nine horses shot out from under him, personally killed thirty Federal troopers during combat, and was himself wounded four times. His daring achievements earned him the rank of lieutenant general and the sole distinction of being the only soldier in either army to be promoted from private to that rank.[23] His exploits won for him the admiring accolades of peers and the begrudging praise of adversaries.

He fought at Shiloh, Chickamauga, Ft. Donnelson, Memphis, and Nashville. His daring successes included the battle ribbons for Brice's Cross Roads where he handsomely defeated a blundering General Sturgis and repaid General Benjamin H. Grierson for the latter's stunning raid into Mississippi a year earlier. Forrest's dogged determination was rewarded by the capture of the Federal raider Colonel Streight and an entire brigade of General Thomas L. Crittenden at Murfreesboro. His exploits included defeating General William Sooy Smith, who was sent expressly by General Sherman to destroy Forrest. General Forrest captured thousands of Union troops and confiscated and destroyed equipment, horses, supplies, and gun boats that ran into the tens of millions of dollars.

At the time Forrest was menacing General Sherman's supply lines at Johnsonville, Sherman referred to him as that "devil Forrest" who for some time Sherman had wanted "hunted down and killed if it costs ten thousand lives and bankrupts the Federal treasury."[24] Eventually General Sherman would be successful in routing Forrest with cavalry under the command of Major General James Harrison Wilson at Selma, Mississippi in 1865.

General Forrest's acclaim as a military leader, as that "Wizzard in the Saddle," cannot be sullied. General William Tecumsah Sherman, no less a gallant, no nonsense, wrathful general, with an equal penchant for destruction and abuse of his adversaries, gave begrudging praise of Forrest. Sherman described the Southern cavalry as "young bloods," "splendid riders, first rate shots, and utterly reckless," "the most dangerous set of men that this war has turned loose upon the world," and led by men like Forrest "are the best cavalry in the world."[25] General Grant proclaimed him "about the ablest cavalry general in the south,"[26] an assessment shared by many in the Confederacy, not the least of whom was President Jefferson Davis.[27]

A distinguished general, Forrest was nevertheless a seething cauldron who when challenged would erupt with reckless violence and abandon. On the battlefield his intuitive instincts and fury could be channeled into novel tactics that outwitted his opponents and obtained for him success. His unbridled energy would carry him personally into the storm of battle with a vengence that could only be satisfied with the complete and unequivocal destruction of his opposition. For Nathan Bedford Forrest, the call to arms was an opportunity to fight the demon within himself, to find release for the inner turmoil. Toward the end of his life he told his lawyer, General John T. Morgan, a U.S. Senator:

> General, I am broken in health and in spirit, and have not long to live. My life has been a battle from the start. It was a fight to achieve a livelihood for those dependent upon me in my younger days, and an independence for myself when I grew up to manhood, as well as in the terrible turmoil of the Civil War. I have seen too much of violence, and I want to close my days at peace with all the world, as I am now at peace with my Maker.[28]

He went to war and spent most of his fortune and sacrificed his health to defend his way of life, to preserve an institution that was his ticket out of the backwoods of poverty, and to rid his country of the pernicious interference of an interloping central government. At Fort Pillow, his inner rage was to reach new heights as the very objects that had contributed to his wealth stood on the parapets. These former chattels, who had been taught to fear him, challenged both the slave trader and the plantation owner. They aroused the deepest anguish and resentment of all who feared the blackman, free and under arms.

The purpose of this treatise is not to discredit General Forrest's military prowess or battlefield successes. Rather, the analysis of General Forrest and Fort Pillow is designed to put in proper focus an incident that grew out of control because Forrest was out of control, and evaluate him, not according to the folk hero he became, but as the man he was.

2

Attack on Fort Pillow

In February 1864, General Sherman's Meridian Expedition was brought to a close. General Sherman designed a two-pronged attack, simultaneously pushing off from Colliersville, east of Memphis, and Vicksburg. The plan anticipated the two forces would link up in Meridian, Mississippi. Sherman expected the operation would gain complete control over the Mississippi interior by destroying the Mobile & Ohio Railroad, paralyzing rebel forces, and undermining Confederate resources and means of communication. General William Sooy Smith was assigned the task of moving south with a force of seven thousand cavalry, and, if the opportunity presented itself, to engage the forces of Nathan Bedford Forrest. Unfortunately, General Smith was decisively defeated at Okolona by General Forrest who commanded half as many troops as his adversary. As General Sherman would acknowledge in later years, the campaign was only a partial success because in the aim to "destroy General Forrest . . . we failed utterly."[1]

In March 1864, General Sherman assumed command of the Military Division of the Mississippi.[2] He became actively engaged in the monumental task of organizing and making preparations for "a large army to move into Georgia, coincident with the advance of the Eastern armies against Richmond."[3] His forces were comprised of components from the armies of the Cumberland, Tennessee, and Ohio. Eventually Sherman's army would number 98,787 troops and contain 254 pieces of artillery and all the wagons and horses necessary to accommodate the proper care for this army. In a communication dated 11 April 1864, he indicated General Grant would be ready to move by 25 April and "when he moves we must."[4]

At this same time, General Forrest's troops were enjoying a period of recuperation and relative calm. Forrest himself had used the period to reorganize his command. General Forrest's reorganization consisted of four brigades and two divisions, which, according to General Orders No. 36 dated 7 March, consisted of the following units.

The First Brigade, Brigadier General R. V. Richarson commanding, contained elements of the Seventh (Colonel W. L. Duckworth), Twelfth (Lieutenant Colonel J. U. Green), Thirteenth (Colonel J. J. Neely), and Fourteenth (Colonel F. M. Stewart) Tennessee regiments.

The Second Brigade, commanded by Colonel Robert McCulloch, was made up of the Second Missouri (Lieutenant Colonel R. A. McCulloch), Willis's Texas battalion (Lieutenant Colonel Leo Willis), First Mississippi Partisans (Major J. M. Parks), Fifth Mississippi Regiment (Major W. B. Perry), Nineteenth Mississippi battalion (Lieutenant Colonel W. L. Duff), Eighteenth Mississippi battalion (Lieutenant Colonel A. H. Chalmers), and McDonald's battalion, which was Forrest's old regiment (Lieutenant Colonel J. M. Crews).

The Third Brigade, commanded by Colonel A. P. Thompson, consisted of the Third (Lieutenant Colonel G. A. C. Holt), Seventh (Colonel Ed Crossland), Eighth (Colonel H. B. Lyon), and Twelfth (Faulkner's) Kentucky regiments, and Jeffrey Forrest's regiment (Lieutenant Colonel D. M. Wisdom).

The Fourth Brigade, commanded by General T. H. Bell, absorbed the Second (Colonel C. R. Barteau), Sixteenth (Colonel A. N. Wilson), and Fifteenth (R. M. Russell) Tennessee regiments.

The First and Second Brigades were formed into one division, which was placed under the command of Brigadier General James R. Chalmers and was known as the First Division of Forrest's Cavalry while the Third and Fourth Brigades were organized into the Second Division under General A. Buford.[5]

On or about 16 March, pursuant to orders, Forrest embarked upon a "short campaign" designated the West Tennessee-Kentucky expedition which was designed to round up conscripts, malingerers, soldiers on unauthorized furloughs, confiscate Federal horses and supplies, and break up lines of communication.[6] In addition, he intended to arrest marauding bands of guerrillas. The Tennessee-Kentucky campaign encompassed an area bounded by the Ohio River in the north and the Mississippi–Tennessee border in the south. It extended in breadth from the Tennessee River in the east to the Mississippi River in the west.

After arriving at Jackson, Tennessee on 20 March, a distance of one hundred fifty miles north of his point of departure—Columbus, Mississippi—Forrest reestablished his headquarters. The march north was not without incident, if only limited to what he saw. "From Tupelo on to Purdy, Tennessee, the country had been laid waste, until there was no longer subsistence for its inhabitants," Forrest reported, "let alone anything to support contemplated troop movements."[7] Besides the "bands and squads of robbers, horse thieves and deserters" actively depleting the resources of the countryside, Forrest was informed about the distressful and abusive conduct of Union Colonel Fielding Hurst's exploits in the area. Lieutenant Colonel W. B. Reed forwarded a report to Forrest's headquarters in Jackson that detailed the numerous infractions committed by the Federals. He accused Colonel Hurst's command of having tortured to death Lieutenant Willis Dodds. It was graphically reported that Dodd's body had been "horribly mutilated" and "barbarously lacerated" and "that his death was brought about by the most inhuman process of torture." In addition, Confederate troopers Alex Vale, Joseph Stewart, John Wilson, and Samuel Osborn of Newsom's Tennessee's volunteer regiment were shot to death after capture by Colonel Hurst's forces as was a Private Martin of Wilson's regiment. A handicapped teenager was also reported to have been "wantonly murdered."[8]

General Forrest sent a dispatch to Brigadier General Buckland, Union Commanding officer at Memphis, demanding the restitution of $5,139.25 "extorted" from Jackson citizens by Colonel Hurst. Further, General Forrest sought the immediate surrender to his custody of Colonel Hurst and those members of his command responsible for the murders; they were to be dealt with according to Confederate authority. He also demanded the release of prominent citizens who were being held at Fort Pillow without charges levied against them. Of particular importance to General Forrest, and, whose specific release he sought, was the Reverend G.W.D. Harris. Forrest threatened to hold five Federal soldiers as hostages for the Reverend's protection and "in case he should die in your hands from ill treatment these men shall be duly executed in retaliation."[9] Not having received a satisfactory response to his demands, General Forrest issued a proclamation dated 22 March in which he declared "Fielding Hurst, and the officers and men of his command, outlaws, and not entitled to be treated as prisoners of war falling into the hands of the forces of the Confederate States."[10] This, of course, meant they could be summarily killed.

Colonel Hurst, for his own safety, was eventually transferred to a different theater of operations, but not until he "was attacked and whipped" by Colonel Neeley of General Chalmers command, in which Colonel Hurst lost 75 men killed and captured, together with the loss of "all his wagons, ambulances, papers and his mistresses, both black and white" and sent "hatless" from the field.[11]

On 23 March Colonel W. L. Duckworth with the Seventh Tennessee Cavalry and Faulkner's regiment proceeded north to Union City, not five miles from the Tennessee/Kentucky border. Union City was garrisoned by about five hundred Union troops. Immediately upon his arrival on the 24th, Colonel Duckworth began to invest the city. After light skirmishing with the pickets, his forces drove the Federals within the protection of their strong fortifications.

Colonel Duckworth, with no artillery on hand, devised a strategy that played heavily on the fears and reservations of Colonel Hawkins, commanding officer of the Federal garrison. Colonel Hawkins' reputation for timidness and lack of daring was well known as he had previously surrendered to General Forrest in December 1862.

> By ingenuous play acting, with horse-holders in the rear raising loud cheers at intervals, as if in welcome to arriving reinforcements, with such sounding of bugles from various points about the town, and with a judicious half display of log "cannon" mounted on wagon wheels and maneuvered about in the bushes in the half-light of dawn, Duckworth managed to create the impression that he had artillery and that reinforcements were continually feeding in. Toward mid morning he sent in his flag of truce with a demand for immediate and unconditional surrender bearing the signature of "N. B. Forrest, Major General commanding."[12]

Characteristic of his mentor Forrest, Colonel Duckworth promised Colonel Hawkins that unless there was an immediate and unconditional surrender he would not be responsible for the garrison's fate. Colonel Hawkins, knowing General Brayman was on his way with reinforcements[13] tried to stall for time by asking to speak with General Forrest himself. Although General Forrest was not on the scene, Colonel Duckworth shrewdly informed Colonel Hawkins that Forrest was not accustomed to speaking with junior officers and if surrender was not forthcoming, the walls would be stormed without sparing any of the defenders. Opting for the kind treatment he had previously received as a prisoner and believing his forces could not sustain an artillery bombardment, Colonel Hawkins surrendered his garrison of 479 mixed troops to the Confederate ruse. He conceded defeat, notwithstanding the fact that two thousand Federals were within six miles of aiding him,[14] the attacking force numbered less than the defenders,[15] and his own men were eager to fight. In subsequent interviews the junior officers of the garrison claimed to have repulsed four initial assaults by the Confederates while suffering only minor casualties.[16]

Following the Confederates' destruction of a railroad bridge on the route to Union City, one military observer insisted "Colonel Hawkins [was] cut off."[17] General Mason Brayman, who commanded the Cairo district, maintained, however, he could have brought the relief column to the garrison if Colonel Hawkins had only held out.[18] The delay caused by the burning bridge effectively prevented General Brayman from reaching the vicinity of Union City before 3:00 P.M., four hours after the surrender.

Owing to the continuing threat of Forrest's forces in that vicinity General Brayman removed the small garrison at Hickman by boat on 24 March.

On 25 March, Forrest and his forces began an investment of Fort Anderson. This garrison was located at Paducah, approximately fifty miles north of Union City. The fort, situated on the western outskirt of town, presented a well-fortified defensive position that was surrounded by a deep ditch with abattis work. With the Ohio River meandering to the rear of the town, two gunboats provided added protection. The post was commanded by Colonel S. G. Hicks, of the Fortieth Illinois Infantry, a resolute and determined officer who estimated his mixed forces at 665.[19] A sharp engagement commenced at 2:00 P.M., which lasted about an hour. Under a flag of truce, the following demand for the fort's surrender was made to Colonel Hicks under the signature of General Forrest.

Colonel: Having a force amply sufficient to carry your works and reduce the place, and in order to avoid the unnecessary effusion of blood, I demand the surrender of the fort and troops, with all public property. If you surrender, you shall be treated as prisoners of war; but if I have to storm your works, you may expect no quarter.[20]

Colonel Hicks replied unequivocally: "I have been placed here by my Government to defend this post, and in this, as well as all other orders from my superiors, I feel it to be my duty as an honorable officer to obey. I must, therefore, respectfully decline surrendering as you may require."[21]

Colonel Hicks reported that during the cessation of hostilities "the enemy were engaged in taking position and planting a bat-

U.S.S. Peosta. Courtesy of the U.S. Army Military History Institute.

tery." After the answer to General Forrest's ultimatum was received, there followed a general engagement in which the Confederate forces were repulsed three times. During this exchange Confederate Colonel A. P. Thompson was killed while impetuously leading a charge upon the works without first having obtained his commanding officer's approval. He, along with many of his men, considered Paducah their home. He was killed when an artillery shell decapitated him. Since Paducah was a heaven for Confederate sympathizers,[22] neither General Brayman nor Colonel Hicks had any regrets for the destruction that occurred to private property. In fact, they were gratified[23] when most of the town was set ablaze from the bombardments of the two gun boats—the *Peosta* and *Paw Paw*—and the intentional efforts of Federal troops who were attempting to dislodge the Confederates who had taken up sniper positions in private residences.[24]

The following day Forrest made a second demonstration against the Federal defenses. Another flag of truce was sent forward for the purpose of exchanging prisoners. This offer was declined by Colonel Hicks. In his report of the encounter, Colonel Hicks observed that of the thirty-five to forty prisoners captured at Paducah by General Forrest, "all of whom, with one exception, were convalescents in the general hospital, and too feeble to get to the fort"[25] when the Federal pickets were initially withdrawn.

Colonel Hicks reported 14 killed and 46 wounded among his

forces. While his estimation of Forrest's losses were excessive at 300 dead and 1,200 wounded, Forrest himself was less than candid in his own report of casualties. On 27 March, he reported his total Tennessee campaign losses "as far as known" at 25 killed and wounded[26] and again on 4 April as 15 killed and 42 wounded. Major Chapman, commanding a detachment of the 122nd Illinois Volunteers at Fort Anderson reported that to his immediate front 15 dead were left behind after the Confederates "moved all the wounded and most of the dead."[27]

Two important considerations are to be noted at this juncture. First, if, in fact, General Forrest sustained more casualties than reflected in his reports, then Colonel Hicks's statement that Forrest admitted to citizens of Paducah "that in no engagement during the war had he been so badly cut up and crippled as at this place"[28] becomes a significant and ominous admission. The losses may have given pause and demonstrated an occurrence "the overly sanguine Confederate had not dreamed possible."[29] Second, the defeat suffered by General Forrest, irrespective of the quantity of supplies he may have come away with and the amount of damage to public property he may have inflicted, could never be taken lightly by the general. Three quarters of General Brayman's aggregate troop strength of 2,329 stationed at Paducah, Cairo, Columbus, Hickman, Island No. 10, and Union City were composed of African Americans.

At Union City the defense by the garrison accorded with General Forrest's estimate that black troops under fire surrender. On the other hand, the defenders at Paducah, approximately two-fifths of whom were African Americans,[30] demonstrated they were not the grateful slaves who had been taught to fear him. Here at Paducah his threats of no quarter were without effect, and the confidence of the commanding officer and the determination of the Union troops drove General Forrest from the field. There would have to be another day to settle this point in General Forrest's mind—another day in which to gather the appropriate trophies.

On 29 March, General Chalmers was ordered to move into Tennessee from Mississippi. He was instructed to deploy his forces between Jackson and Memphis and to keep Forrest apprised of any movements made by the Federals.[31] On 4 April, General Forrest reported "There is a Federal force of 500 to 600 at Fort Pillow, which I shall attend to in a day or two, as they have horses and supplies which we need."[32] The following day General Buford was directed to proceed with his forces against Columbus and

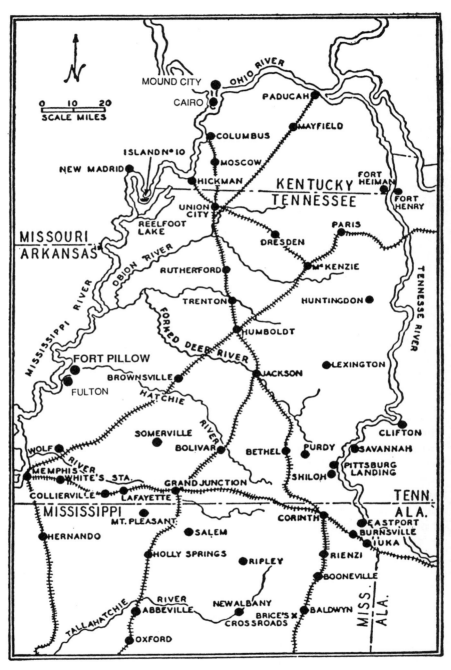

West Tennessee and Kentucky, 1864. Courtesy of William Konecky Associates.

Paducah. A demonstration by Colonel Neely's brigade at Memphis and General Buford's advance against the outposts at Columbus and Paducah were designed to deceive the Federals as to Forrest's real intention of assailing Fort Pillow.[33]

A detachment of General Buford's troops arrived at Columbus on 12 April. The following day, after driving in the Federal pickets, the customary ultimatum was sent. The fort was to be surrendered or no quarter would be given its occupants. Under General Buford's signature, the note read as follows:

> Fully capable of taking Columbus and its garrison by force, I desire to avoid the shedding of blood and therefore demand the unconditional surrender of the forces under your command. Should you surrender, the negroes now in arms will be returned to their masters. Should I, however, be compelled to take the place, no quarter will be shown to the negro troops whatever; the white troops will be treated as prisoners of war.[34]

Colonel William Hudson Lawrence, commander of the post, defiantly answered with the following dispatch.

> Your communication of this date is to hand. In reply I would state that, being placed by my Government with adequate force to hold and repel all enemies from my post, surrender is out of the question.[35]

At the time this encounter was taking place, General Buford was marching his remaining forces to Paducah. Upon deploying his troops he, too, sent Colonel Hicks the usual demand and, in stalling for time, suggested women, children, and noncombatants be permitted an hour to seek safer ground. The stalwart Colonel Hicks agreed with the procedure to protect civilians and then dared General Buford to come ahead as he was ready.[36] General Buford chose instead to steal one hundred fifty horses and keep the Union garrison occupied within the breastworks of their fort.

With several of his units engaged in separate operations, General Forrest succeeded with his plans for diversion and preoccupying the various Federal forces. Potential Union reinforcements were deployed many miles north of Fort Pillow. Memphis, with hysterical urgency, was preparing for an anticipated assault by the Confederates. After the battle of Paducah, on 26 March, the overconfident General Brayman wrote: "Do not think there need be any apprehension regarding Fort Pillow."[37]

The way was now open to attack Fort Pillow with impunity.

Fort Pillow was situated along the eastern shore of the Missis-

Main river battery at Fort Pillow, 1862. This artist's sketch appeared in *The Illustrated London News,* **12 July 1862.**

sippi River about thirty-five miles due north of Memphis. The fort was built by General Gideon J. Pillow, commander of the Confederate forces of Tennessee in 1861.[38] The general chose the location for the fort because its strategic command of the Mississippi River would enhance the defenses of Memphis and thwart Union naval activity on the waterway. Following the Battle of Shiloh in 1862, General Beauregard, however, was constrained to evacuate his troops from Corinth. At that time, with General McClernand's Federal troops advancing toward Memphis, the occupation of Fort Pillow was no longer tenable. It was abandoned by the Confederates on 1 June 1862.[39]

The fort was located atop a high clay bluff or bank that ascended from the river's edge some seventy-five to one hundred feet in a steep incline. Reaching out from the opposite bank along the Arkansas shore was a natural sandbar that stretched nearly across the entire width of the river. During low water periods "this obstruction to navigation was for several months of each year many feet above the surface of the river, and spreads out, a flat, monotonous plain, as dry and verdureless as a patch of Libyan Desert"[40] thereby causing river traffic to operate close to the banks of the Tennessee side. The proximity of boats to the shore while traversing this obstacle and the height of the fortifications created an ominous deterrent to any navigation passing this point.

The total configuration of the fort was triangular in shape. The outer exterior trenches reached from Cold Creek, which abutted the fort's northeasterly boundary and flowed into the river, in a slightly bowed or arching shape southward below the fort to the Mississippi River. In length, the outer trench was over two miles long. Six hundred yards inside this outer trench an interior work was erected. This trench or fortification was equally distant from the river and the outer entrenchment and zigzagged along the "crest of a commanding hill."[41] Three hundred yards closer to the river and on top of the bluff itself was the main fortification. Beginning at the confluence of Cold Creek and the Mississippi River, this area was constructed in a horseshoe or semicircular form and was about seventy yards at its widest point. Several yards outside the breastworks were two rifle pits nestled near the edge of the bluff. Outside the northeast and southern extremities of the main fortification and perpendicular to the creek and river were two deep ravines almost encircling the fort.[42] One was the Cold Creek Ravine and was unoccupied; the other ran two hundred yards inland and four hundred fifty feet from the redoubt walls, and sheltered in two rows the hospital, hotel, storehouses, sutler cabins, quartermaster building, and shacks that contributed to the life of the garrison. Within the main fortification, near the edge of the bluff, the black troops slept on straw in planked floor tents. The white troops bivouaced on bunks in the out buildings or barracks arranged in rows located outside the breastworks on the ridge that gently slopped to the ravine south of the bluff. At the water's edge, about a hundred feet from the fort's rear exposure was a steamboat wharf. The earth wall that constituted the parapet was six feet high, eight feet in depth, and four feet across the top. This structure contained six embrasures that allowed placement for the cannons that were aimed to cover the approaches to the fort. Directly in front of this wall was a ledge that fell off sharply to a ditch twelve feet wide and eight feet deep with perpendicular walls. "A deep ravine surrounded the fort and from the fort to the ravine the ground descends rapidly."[43] Inside the parapet, and lining its entire 120-yard facing was a bench upon which the defenders could ascend when ready to fire. This enclosure afforded the men relative safety below the head and shoulders when firing their rifles.

The ground in front of the fortification had been mostly

Interior of restored fortifications.

cleared of standing timber by thousands of slaves during the Confederate occupation. The character of the terrain was interspersed with numerous knolls of various heights, some as high as the fort itself, and marked with hollows and depressions. While most of the trees had been taken down and the original underbrush cut away, stumps and logs remained and new underbrush had reappeared by April 1864.

According to a report dated 26 April from Lieutenant Colonel and Assistant Adjutant-General T. H. Harris, the garrison was believed to have had a troop compliment of 557 officers and men.[44] This figure, used by many early writers, is now generally understood to have been erroneously based on imprecise and incomplete morning reports. The author has calculated the total troop strength at 578, although arguably the figure may have been as high as 585. Since Major Bradford conducted recruitment from the fort it is entirely possible, as two historians suggest, that the actual number of white troops included recent inductees for whom no official records can be found as a result of the fire that destroyed the garrison's papers. The approximate figures contained in this text may be stated as follows: First Battalion, Sixth U.S. Heavy Artillery (colored), 8 commissioned and 250 enlisted

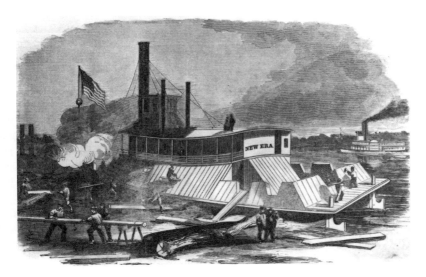

U.S.S. New Era. **Courtesy of the Library of Congress.**

men; one section, Company D, Second U.S. Light Artillery (colored), 1 commissioned officer and 34 men;[45] First Battalion, Thirteenth Tennessee Cavalry, Major William F. Bradford, commanding, 10 commissioned officers and 275 enlisted men. Nine known civilian fighters are excluded from this count although one was killed and several wounded.[46] The field pieces at the post consisted of two 6-pounders, two 12-pounders and two-10 pound Parrotts. Lieutenant Colonel Harris's aggregate estimate of black and white troops did not account for the fact that except in rare instances all officers in black units were white. Therefore, the total composition of the several units was approximately 284 black enlistees and 294 white officers and men.

On station in the river was the gun boat *New Era,* captained by James Marshall. The *New Era* was a 157 ton, wooden-hulled, wood burning steamer with a four-foot draft. The converted river ferry was 137 feet long and about 30 feet wide, reinforced with heavy timber. Her decks contained three 24-pound howitzers on each of the port and starboard sides. The gun boat's speed was approximately seven knots against the current of the Mississippi River. In charge of the garrison was Major Lionel F. Booth, a native of Philadelphia, who had enlisted in the regular army in 1858 at the age of twenty. As was common during the time of recruiting black units, experienced and worthy white soldiers volunteered to serve with these units because of the promotional opportunities such assignments afforded. For the most part, these officers demonstrated a deep commitment to the effort of raising black units. Booth transferred in 1863 to the Sixth USCHA where he rose to the rank of Major. On 28 March 1864, ironically the day after he applied for a furlough,[47] Major Booth was ordered to Fort Pillow by Major General Hurlbut, commander of all volunteer forces in and about Memphis. Major Booth was to take command of the post from Major William F. Bradford who was stationed there with elements of the Thirteenth Tennessee Cavalry. Major Booth was directed to confer "freely and fully with Major Bradford, . . . whom [he would] find a good officer, though not of much experience."[48]

General Hurlbut, an attorney from Charleston, South Carolina, saw service in the Mexican War. He had a dubious military reputation despite his combat experience. Hurlbut acquired his military experience with General Sherman at the Battle of Shiloh and during the Meridian Campaign. Thereafter, General Sherman assigned General Hurlbut to the West Tennessee Command in charge of volunteers with headquarters in Memphis. These volunteers consisted mainly of runaway or emancipated slaves and whites from West Tennessee.

In response to an inquiry to observe General Hurlbut's fitness for command, General Sherman remembered describing him, unflatteringly, as "far above the average in the knowledge of regimental and brigade drill."[49] On 11 April 1864 Sherman wrote General Hurlbut expressing his opinion that while the latter had a "high order of professional knowledge . . . I do not think you inclined to the rough contact of field service." His execution of orders was considered "not so good," and Sherman advised Hurlbut that General Grant thought Hurlbut clung "too close to Memphis from a love of ease, or other reason."[50] Although Sherman knew "we must now have men of action," it was not until after the Fort Pillow disaster that General Hurlbut was removed from the Memphis command.

General Hurlbut operated under the mistaken belief that Fort Pillow's commanding positions could "be held by a small force against any odds." He advised Major Booth that Forrest's "check at Paducah" would cause him to "fall back to Jackson and thence across the Tennessee [river]" and not "try the river again." He did warn Major Booth to put the "works into perfect order and the post into its strongest defense."[51] This dispatch may have in part prompted Major Booth's communication of 3 April wherein

Site where Federal pickets were attacked.

he confidently but mistakenly reported he had no apprehensions or fear the fort would be attacked or threatened. His opinion that Fort Pillow was "perfectly safe,"[52] and he could hold the fort for forty-eight hours[53] proved to be a fatal miscalculation.

In the early morning of 12 April, General James R. Chalmers arrived at the outer reaches of the fort with a force comprised of McCulloch's brigade and Colonel T. H. Bell's brigade of General Buford's division. General Chalmers had moved due west at 3:30 P.M. from Brownsville the previous day, covering a distance of forty miles in about fourteen hours. According to General Chalmers, McCulloch's advance at 6:00 A.M. along the northern portion of the outer entrenchments drove in the Federal pickets and succeeded in capturing four. The main garrison had been awake only a short time, preparing for roll call and breakfast, when the first sounds of musketry were heard.

In the absence of General Forrest, but responding to the general's prior orders, General Chalmers proceeded to invest the garrison. "McCulloch's brigade moved down the Fulton road to Gaines' farm; thence north to the fort on a road running parallel with the Mississippi River; Wilson's regiment, of Bell's brigade, moved on a direct road from Brownsville to Fort Pillow, and Colonel Bell with Barteau's and Russell's regiments moved down Coal Creek to attack the fort in the rear."[54]

The fort unleashed a furious artillery barrage. Companies D and E previously sent from the fort to check the Confederate advance withdrew from the foremost rifle pits.

"The firing continued without cessation" reported Federal Lieutenant Leaming, "principally from behind logs, stumps and under cover of thick underbrush and from high knolls until 9 A.M., when the rebels made a general assault on our works, which was successfully repulsed with severe loss to them and but slight loss to our garrison. We, however, suffered pretty severely in the loss of command officers by the unerring aim of the rebel sharpshooters."[55] At this time, nine o'clock, while directing his troops, Major Booth was mortally struck by a bullet piercing his heart. The next ranking officer, Major Bradford, assumed command.

Lieutenant Leaming's report continued:

> At about 11 A.M., the rebels made a second determined assault on our works. In this attempt they were again successfully repulsed with severe loss. The enemy succeeded, however, in obtaining possession of two rows of barracks running parallel to the south side of the fort and distant 150 yards. The barracks had previously been ordered to be destroyed, but after severe loss on our part in the attempt to execute the order our men were compelled to retire without accomplishing the desired end, save only the row nearest to the fort. From these barracks the enemy kept up a murderous fire on our men, despite all our efforts to dislodge him.
>
> Owing to the close proximity of these buildings to the fort, and to the fact that they were on considerably lower ground, our artillery could not be sufficiently depressed to destroy them, or even render them untenable for the enemy. Musketry and artillery firing continued, however, on both sides with great energy, and although our garrison was completely surrounded, all attempts of the enemy to carry our works by assault were successfully repulsed, notwithstanding his great superiority in numbers.

During all this time the gun boat *New Era* kept up a constant fire, lobbing five-inch shells and shrapnel in an attempt to enfilade the Confederate positions. Receiving signal direction from a flag officer located at the rear of the fort, these efforts for the most part were ineffectual in causing either dislodgment of the enemy or casualties. At best, the *New Era* succeeded in causing the rebels to move from one protected ravine or knoll to another. Lieutenant Leaming stated the *New Era* was able to render but little assistance owing to the high bluff and long range required of its shot. Forrest concurred the gun boat's continuous fire "was without effect."[56] The *New Era* reported to have successfully removed in the morning a barge containing such of the females and other noncombatants who desired to leave. These were towed above Coal Creek. Shortly thereafter, some of the them climbed aboard the steamer *Liberty*, which, in passing the fort, was subjected to fire. At noon, Captain Marshall reported the enemy was firing on him. He claims all firing ceased at 1:45 P.M. when a flag of truce was sent in and not resumed until 3:15 P.M.[57]

General Forrest, who had not initially been on the field, arrived at 10:00 A.M. and proceeded to direct the movement of his troops. Before the fighting was to end, he would have three horses shot from underneath him. He directed and cautioned his troops to make good use of the excellent cover provided by the terrain, fallen timber, and underbrush. Riflemen posted on top of the knolls were able to pin down the fort's defenders who would have to expose themselves on top of the earthworks in order to effectively fire down on the advancing Confederates. Forrest's troops ensconced themselves in the Coal Creek ravine and among the barracks at the southern extremity of the fort. Colonel Barteau, moving steathly along the Coal Creek bluff was able to deploy his men within the ravine, though not without some casualties. At this point he was seventy-five yards from the fort but sufficiently beneath the earthwork to be practically immune from the firing of the fort.

In his official report Forrest stated the following:

> Assuming command, I ordered General Chalmers to advance his lines and gain position on the slope, where our men would be perfectly protected from the heavy fire of artillery and musketry, as the enemy could not depress their pieces so as to rake the slopes, nor could they fire on them with small-arms except by mounting the breast-works and exposing themselves to the fire of our sharpshooters, who, under cover of stumps and logs, forced them to keep down inside the works. After several hours' hard fighting the desired position was gained, not, however, without considerable loss. Our main line was now within an average distance of 100 yards from the fort, and exended from Coal Creek on the right to the bluff, or bank, of the Mississippi River on the left.[58]

General Chalmers similarly described the events leading up to the truce.

> The fight was opened at daylight by McCulloch. He moved cautiously through the ravines and short hills which encompassed the

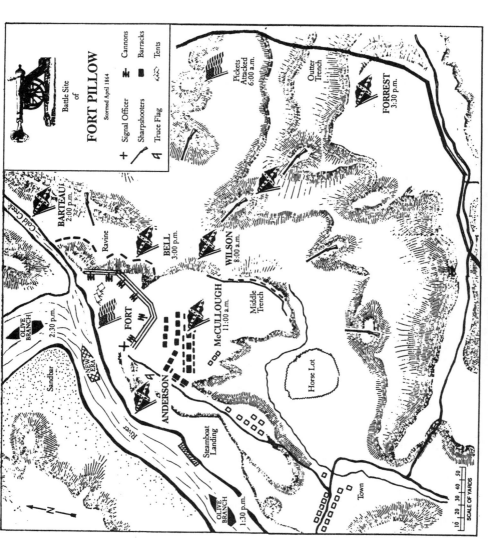

Fort Pillow battle illustration. Courtesy of Action Advertising.

place, protecting the men as much as possible from the enemy's artillery, five pieces of which from the fort aided by two gun-boats[59] on the
river, played furiously upon him. Moving in this manner he succeeded
about 11 o'clock in taking the work [middle trenches], which I have
spoken of as having been commenced by General Villepigue, and
the flag of the Eighteenth Mississippi Battalion, Lieutenant-Colonel
Chalmers commanding, which had been the first regiment to enter
the fort, was quickly flying above it.

While Colonel McCulloch had been moving up on the left, Colonel
Bell moved up on the right and rear, and Colonel Wilson moved up
on the center, taking advantage of the ground as much as possible to
shelter their men. Affairs were in this condition, with the main fort
completely invested, when Major-General Forrest arrived with Colonel Wisdom's regiment of Buford's division. After carefully examining
the position he ordered a general charge to be made. The troops
responded with alacrity and enthusiasm, and in a short time took
possession of all the rifle-pits around the fort, and closed up on all
sides within 25 or 30 yards of the outer ditch. Here a considerable
delay occurred from the ammunition being exhausted. A supply, however, was obtained as quickly as possible from the ordnance train and
everything was made ready for another advance.[60]

Major Charles W. Anderson, then a captain and aide-de-camp
to General Forrest, indicated that by one o'clock the Federals were
driven within the fort's main fortifications. He claimed the rebel
"lines were formed extending from Coal Creek on the right to the
landing on the bank of the Mississippi River on the left, varying in
distance from 50 to 150 yards of the works." The fort was entirely
surrounded with Barteau's regiment on the right and rear and
three companies of McCulloch's command in old rifle pits on the
left and rear.

The width or thickness of the works across the top prevented the
garrison from firing down on us, as it could only be done by mounting
and exposing themselves to unerring aim of our sharpshooters,
posted behind stumps and logs on all the neighboring hills. They were
also unable to depress their artillery so as to rake these slopes with
grape and canister, and so far as safety was concerned, we were as
well fortified as they were; the only difference was that they were on
one side and we on the other of the same fortification. They had no
sharpshooters with which to annoy our main force, while ours sent a
score of bullets at every head that appeared above the walls.

Our heaviest loss was in gaining this position, and when gained it
was perfectly apparent to any man endowed with the smallest amount
of common sense, that to all intents and purposes the fort was ours.[61]

Lieutenant Leaming reported that at 3:30 P.M. the firing ceased at the appearance of a white flag. At one hundred fifty yards from the fort's southern extremity, the party bearing the truce was halted and Captains Bradford and Young, together with Lieutenant Leaming, were ordered out to receive the communication. The communication, signed by General Forrest, was examined within the fort. This first message, according to Major Charles W. Anderson, read as follows:

> Headquarters Forrest's Cavalry—Before Fort Pillow, April 12, 1864.
> Major Booth: The conduct of the officers and men garrisoning Fort Pillow has been such as to entitle them to being treated as prisoners of war. I demand the unconditional surrender of the garrison, promising that you shall be treated as prisoners of war. My men have received a fresh supply of ammunition, and from their present position, can easily assault and capture the fort. Should my demand be refused, I cannot be responsible for the fate of your command.[62]

Essentially, this statement accorded with Leaming's recollection of the message, except that Leaming remembered the last line as "and if compelled to do so [assault the works] you must take the consequences."[63]

The fort's response contained the following language:

> Headquarters U.S. Forces,
> Fort Pillow, Tenn., April 12, 1864
>
> Major General N. B. Forrest,
> Commanding Confederate Cavalry:
>
> General: Yours of this instant is received, and in reply I have to ask one hour for consultation and consideration with my officers and the officers of the gun-boat.
> Very respectfully, your obedient servant.
> L. F. Booth
> Major, Commanding U.S. Forces

Anderson's report of this correspondence, claimed to have been copied from originals in his possession, reflected the same context, but he wrote the Booth message contained the understanding that "(i)n the meantime no preparation to be made on either side."[64] At the time these messages were exchanged Major Booth had been dead several hours. For reasons of strategy the remaining officers of the fort deemed it "proper and advisable" that the Confederates not be apprised of Major Booth's death.

Leaming returned to the fort and within a few minutes another message was delivered under a flag of truce. Anderson quoted the communication as follows:

> Headquarters Forrest's Cavalry
> Before Fort Pillow, April 12, 1864
>
> Major L. F. Booth,
> Commanding U.S. Forces, Fort Pillow:
> Sir: I have the honor to acknowledge the receipt of your note, asking one hour to consider my demand for your surrender. Your request cannot be granted. I will allow you twenty minutes from the receipt of this note for consideration: if at the expiration of that time the fort is not surrendered, I shall assault it. I do not demand the surrender of the gun boat.
> Very respectfully,
> N. B. Forrest
> Major-General

Lieutenant Leaming related that during this last exchange an officer galloped up and said "That gives you twenty minutes to surrender; I am General Forrest."[65] Whether as a result of prior misinformation concerning Forrest's location or of not seeing him present in the early stages of the conflict, the ranking Federal officers did not believe Forrest was on the field until this exchange.

During the cessation of firing the attention of the garrison was primarily directed to the south of the fort where the truce communications were being received. While the negotiations were in process, Forrest "took occasion to move his troops, partially under cover of a ravine and thick underbrush, into the very position he had been fighting to obtain throughout the entire engagement."[66] Lieutenant Leaming severely censured and rebuked Forrest for having "resorted to means the most foul and infamous ever adopted" by these deployments. Another officer, who was taken prisoner and escaped, Second Lieutenant Van Horn, confirmed that during the truce consultations "advantage was taken by the enemy to place in position his force, they crawling up to the fort."[67] Following receipt of the Confederate ultimatum to surrender, the officers of the garrison unanimously voted not to strike the colors. Consistent with the feigned authority previously used and characterized by a curt military chivalry, the written reply simply stated: "General: I will not surrender. Very respectfully, your obedient servant. L. F. Booth, Commanding U.S. Forces, Fort Pillow."

Within minutes of receiving the garrison's reply, General For-

Interior of restored fortifications.

rest ordered an assault all along his lines. As the bugler "Gus" sounded the charge, a seething passion was to explode, tearing away at the very core of human dignity. Above the din of musketry and cannon fire came the piercing yell of the rebels, who, "as if rising from out the very earth on the center and north side, within 20 yards of our works, the rebels received our first fire, wavered, rallied again and finally succeeded in breaking our lines, and thus gaining possession of the fort."[68] All the ugliness of hate raged in the bosoms of the attackers; an uncontrolled conflagration fanned by the sight of defiant Negroes in arms standing shoulder to shoulder with "renegade Tennesseans."

The Confederates were to enter the "great slaughter pen"[69] and cause the Mississippi River to flow "crimsoned with the red blood of the flying foe."[70] The contest was no longer a battle between warring factions in a civilized country. Forrest's men were "sharing in a race riot, a mass lynching, and the event became an orgy of unleashed primitive human animals riding a storm of anger and vengeance directed at their sworn enemy, whom they considered less than human and beyond all laws of civilized war: the negro."[71]

Kurz and Allison Chromolithograph. Courtesy of Anne S. K. Brown Military Collection, Brown University Library.

The carnage of this bloody engagement and the toll of human suffering were unparalleled at this juncture of the Civil War. Clearly major battles such as Gettysburg, Fredericksburg, Antietem, and Shiloh had conditioned the public to casualty figures of frightening proportions and battle scenes of gruesome detail. Undoubtedly, there were isolated instances of excess, but nothing that approached the killing fields of Fort Pillow. The extraordinary aspect of the Fort Pillow incident is to be found in the wanton disregard for any degree of civility, even as that term may have limited application to the reality of war, and the savagery and vicious brutality practiced by the victors.

Numerous accounts of the affair graphically portrayed a macabre scene. These descriptions, in the main obtained from the statements of eyewitnesses, contain a certain quality of emotion and, in some respects, exaggeration and errant factual detail. For those asked to describe their personal experiences within days of the incident, little defense need be proffered for their expressive language. Estimates relating to the aggregate number of attacking forces in the vicinity of six to seven thousand is concededly incorrect. The generally accepted figure for Forrest's forces arrayed before Fort Pillow on 12 April 1864 is fifteen to eighteen hundred.

Several references to the time specific events occurred also contain discrepancies. The facts indicate that the attack opened at 6:00 A.M. on Tuesday, 12 April, with fighting slackening at about 1:00 P.M. and possibly, except for sporadic fire, ceasing. The truce occurred at about 3:00 P.M. with the final assault commencing at 3:30 and lasting approximately twenty to thirty minutes. The number of prisoners taken also varies between several accounts owing to incomplete information and limited exposure to the whole scene as observed by these witnesses. Additionally, estimates by several witnesses that they personally saw at least a hundred killed, is no doubt exaggerated with respect to their individual observations. The number of dead after the fort's defenses were breached and the troops retreated down the bluff must have been in the vicinity of two hundred to two hundred and twenty, excluding civilian casualties. The precise number of killed and wounded suffered by the garrison before the final assault cannot be ascertained with any degree of reliability. Survivor accounts place the number of killed at about twenty. It is reasonable to assume that whatever number of casualties were inflicted at that time, the officers believed the garrison had sufficient manpower available for an adequate and continued defense.

A civilian, Elois Bevel, had arrived at the fort from Arkansas the evening preceding the attack. He claimed to have been in a good position south of the fort to see the Confederates using the truce to consolidate their position and witnessed "the Union soldiers, black and white, slaughtered while asking for quarter."[72] Mr. James R. Bingham, a clerk in a store at Fort Pillow, claimed "as soon as the Confederates got into the fort, the Federals threw down their arms in token of surrender," and despite shouts of "we surrender," an "indiscriminate massacre commenced."[73] He estimated between 20 and 25 had been killed and 15 wounded prior to the final assault. He "heard officers say they would never recognize negroes as prisoners of war, but would kill them whenever taken," and the officers of these troops would be treated the same. After being picked up by a gunboat, he was returned to the fort. He recognized the remains of Lieutenant Ackerstrom "nailed to a house, and supposed burned alive." He also observed the remains of two Negroes lying where the house burned, and he was informed that they, too, were pinioned to the floor.[74]

The appearance of Lieutenant Ackerstrom was confirmed by

Fort Pillow Massacre. Appeared in Frank Leslie's Illustrated Newspaper.

the wife of Thomas Rufins.[75] This "spectacle" of Lt. Ackerstrom "nailed to the side of the house" was also viewed by two other trooper wives: Rebecca Williams and Nancy Hopper.[76]

Hardin Cason, Company A, Sixth U.S. Heavy Artillery, swore he witnessed wounded Corporal Robert Winston murdered by a rebel soldier.[77] The affidavit of Corporal Cothel stated he was shot through the arm after being taken a prisoner, and he allegedly saw seventeen others wounded while prisoners.[78] William Dickey of the Thirteenth Tennessee Cavalry saw the enemy gain positions under the flag of truce which they had not previously obtained. He certified he saw Negroes thrown into the river, and "while struggling for life," shot. Along with ten others he was shot "while I had my hands up begging for mercy."[79] Elias Falls, also of Company A, was ordered with several others to march up the hill, where they were fired upon while marching.[80] Daniel Ranker confirmed the shooting of black troops in the water.[81]

Jason Souden, Company B, Thirteenth Tennessee Cavalry, also confirmed the enemy made use of the flag of truce to advance their forces and that he was shot after he surrendered. He claimed the Federals ran down the bluff when it was apparent no quarter was to be given. He saw the rebels kill Sergeant Gwaltney of Company B, with his own revolver, shot twice in the head. He certified that the following day the rebels "dispatched" several of the wounded blacks.[82] Shooting of the wounded the day after the attack was also confirmed by Emanuel Nichols.[83]

William Mays, also of Company B, stated in his affidavit:

> We all threw down our arms and gave tokens of surrender, asking for quarter (I was wounded in the right shoulder and muscle of the back and knocked down before I threw down my gun). But no quarter was given. Voices were heard upon all sides, crying "Give them no quarter: kill them: kill them: it is General Forrest's orders." I saw 4 white men and at least 25 negroes shot while begging for mercy, and I saw 1 negro dragged from a hallow log within 10 feet of where I lay, and as 1 rebel held him by the foot another shot him. These were all soldiers. There were also 2 negro women and 3 little children standing within 25 steps from me, when a rebel stepped up to them and said, "Yes, God damn you, you thought you were free, did you?" and shot them all. They all fell but 1 child, when he knocked it in the head with the breech of his gun. They then disappeared in the direction of the landing, following up the fugitives, firing at them wherever seen. They came back in about three-quarters of an hour shooting and robbing the dead of their money and clothes. I saw a man with a canteen upon him and a pistol in his hand. I ventured to ask him for a drink of water. He turned around, saying, "Yes, God damn you, I will give you a drink of water" and shot at my head three different times covering my face up with dust, and then turned from me—no doubt thinking he had killed me—remarking "God damn you, it's too late to pray now"; then went on with his pilfering.[84]

Hardy N. Revelle, a dry goods clerk who participated in the fort's defense as a sharpshooter, saw two white men in a ravine with the garrison's surgeon Dr. Fitch. Revelle was halfway down the hill when he observed the two men fix a white handkerchief to a stump and raise their hands. They were shot and killed despite their efforts to gain quarter.

> When we found there was no quarter to be shown, and that (white and black) we were to be butchered, we also gave up our arms and passed down the hill. It is stated, at this time, Major Bradford put a white handkerchief on his sword-point and waived it in token of submission, but it was not heeded if he did. . . .
> A captain of the rebel troops then came where we were and ordered all the Federals (white and black) to move up the hill or he would "shoot their God-damned brains out." I started up the hill with a number of others in accordance with the order. I was surrendered with our men. While going up I saw white men fall on both sides of me, who were shot down by rebel soldiers who were stationed upon the brow of the hill. We were at the time marching directly toward

the men who fired upon us. I do not know how many fell, but I remember of seeing 4 killed in this way. I also saw negroes shot down with pistols in the hands of rebels. One was killed at my side. I saw another negro struck on the head with a saber by a rebel soldier. I suppose he was also killed. One more just in front of me was knocked down with the butt of a musket. We kept on up the hill. I expected each moment to meet my fate with the rest.

At the top of the hill I met a man named Cutler, a citizen of Fort Pillow. He spoke to a rebel captain about me, and we then went under orders from the captain to one of the stores under the hill, where the captain got a pair of boots. This was about 4 P.M. on Tuesday.

I am positive that up to the time of the surrender there had not been more than 50 men (black and white) killed and wounded on the Union side. Of these but about 20 had been among the killed. The balance of all killed and wounded on our side were killed and wounded after we had given undoubted evidence of a surrender, and contrary to all rules of warfare.[85]

Daniel Stamps, Company E, Thirteenth Tennessee Cavalry, claimed after the Federals had given way at the fort's parapet, the troops ran down the bluff saying "the rebels were showing no quarter."

I then threw down my gun and ran down with them, closely pursued by the enemy shooting down every man black and white. They said they had orders from Forrest to show no quarter, but to "kill the last god damn one of them." While I was standing at the bottom of the hill, I heard a rebel officer shout out an order of some kind to the men who had taken us, and saw a rebel soldier standing by me. I asked him what the officer had said. He repeated it to me again. It was, "kill the last damn one of them." The soldier replied to his officer that we had surrendered; that we were prisoners and must not be shot. The officer again replied, seeming crazy with rage that he had not been obeyed, "I tell you to kill the last God damned one of them." He then turned and galloped off. I also certify that I saw 2 men shot down while I was under the bluff. They fell nearly at my feet. They had their hands up; had surrendered, and were begging for mercy. I do also certify that on the ensuing morning I saw negroes who were wounded, and had survived the night, shot and killed as fast as they could be found. One rebel threatened to kill me because I would not tell him where a poor negro soldier was who had been wounded badly, but who had crawled off on his hands and knees and hidden behind a log. I was myself also shot some two hours after I had surrendered.[86]

James Taylor, also of Company E, related in his sworn statement:

I was shot after I had surrendered, and while going down the bluff. I also saw them shoot down about 12 colored soldiers, and that after they had surrendered. Some were on their knees with outstretched hands, begging for mercy. . . . I also saw on the next morning, the 13th of April 1864, the rebels come upon the ground and kill all the wounded they could find. I saw them make 2 of the wounded negroes stand upon their feet that they might see them fall again when shot; and shot they were.[87]

William Walker, of the Thirteenth Tennessee Cavalry was shot in the left eye after giving up his money. He stated:

The rebels had almost ceased firing upon us when an officer came down and told them to "Shoot the last damned one of us," and "not to take one prisoner." He said it was the orders of the general (I could not hear the name plainly, but I think it was Chalmers). Then the slaughter of the prisoners was resumed. I saw some 6 white and 10 colored soldiers thus shot, long after they had surrendered, and while the negroes were on their knees begging to be spared.[88]

Private Sandy Addison and Sergeant Wilbur Gaylord, both of the Sixth U.S. Heavy Artillery had been taken prisoner; Addison escaped and Gaylord was paroled. Each trooper testified they saw or heard other prisoners had been shot. Sergeant Gaylord estimated ten men were killed prior to the flag of truce. He claimed a Texas ranger spared him and a black soldier.[89] A private in Company B of the same regiment, George Huston, claimed after the fort was taken the troops "took refuge under [the] river bank" where a corporal and/or sergeant raised a white flag that was given no consideration since an officer indicated it was General Forrest's order to kill the blacks. Private James Lewis of the same regiment confirmed the presence of a white flag being raised at the water's edge. He also observed the shooting of two women "and their bodies thrown into the river."[90]

The first sergeant of Company C, Sixth U.S. Heavy Artillery, Henry F. Weaver, was stationed at one of the two 10-pound Parrott guns which were placed in battery at the south end of the works. About noon, after the rebels received reinforcements, he observed them "advancing close to the fort getting into the houses of the cavalry and some rifle-pits we had made a few days before, and which proved of more use to them than us, and kept up such a brisk fire that it was almost impossible to work the guns." Owing to poor fuses he calculated that not more than one in five shells burst. After the truce was in effect he observed the rebels took advantage of the truce and moved up close under our works, and took their positions ready for a charge. The demand to surrender was refused, and up to this time but few had been killed but a good many wounded; but now the charge came, and as they came up they gave their usual yell, and the Thirteenth Cavalry fled for the banks of the river. When the cavalry commenced to break our colored men wavered, and the rebels had by this time succeeded in entering the fort. Lieutenant Van Horn begged and ordered them to stop, but each one sought safety in flight, as the rebels had commenced an indiscriminate slaughter of the black soldiers, and as far as I could see, every one was shot down so close to me that they would nearly fall on me. I surrendered, the rebel remarking that they did not shoot white men, but wanted to know what in hell I was there fighting with the damned nigger for. I soon got away from him, for he was too intent on murder to mind me; but had gone but a few steps when another rebel met me and demanded my greenbacks, and after robbing me of everything but my clothes he left me as not worthy of his further notice. I then went down the river to the quartermaster's house, where I found Lieutenant Van Horn. We stayed there about ten minutes, when a rebel came in and again demanded our surrender. I told him I had done so twice already. He then ordered us to follow him. We did, going up into town and into a store, where he commenced to pillage and I to get on some citizen's clothing, which I soon did, and got out of the store. I now missed Lieutenant Van Horn, and did not see him again until the next Sunday, when I found he had escaped and got back to Fort Pickering before me. Companies B and D were outside the fort in the rifle-pits until the enemy received his re-enforcements, when they retired inside of the fort. Major Booth, from the time he took command of the post at Fort Pillow, was strengthening the same by throwing up rifle-pits, building platforms, and making embrasures in the fort for the purpose of working his guns. I succeeded in making my escape by getting citizen's clothing and playing off as rebel. I then hid myself under the bank of the river until a tug-boat came along, which I boarded.[91]

Private Jacob Wilson identified five members of his outfit, Company B, of the Sixth U.S. Heavy Artillery, whom he saw shot by the rebels after they surrendered.

Lieutenant Leaming, whose written report was dated after he testified before the Committee on the Conduct of the War, described being wounded after the surrender and offered his assessment for "this horrid work of butchery," which was renewed again the next morning, "when numbers of our wounded were basely murdered after a long night of pain and suffering on the field where they had fought so bravely."

The rebels were very bitter against these loyal Tennesseans, terming them "home-made Yankees," and declaring they would give them no better treatment than they dealt to the Negro troops with whom they were fighting.

In estimating the number killed, which must have included civilians, he claimed: "Of the number, white and black, actually murdered after the surrender I cannot say positively; however, from my own observation, as well as from prisoners who were captured at Fort Pillow and afterward made their escape, I cannot estimate that number at anything less than 300."

He further stated,

> the bravery of our troops in the defense of Fort Pillow, I think, cannot be questioned. Many of the men, and particularly the colored soldiers, had never before been under fire;[92] yet every man did his duty with a courage and determined resolution, seldom if ever surpassed in similar engagements. Had Forrest not violated the rules of civilized warfare in taking advantage of the flag of truce in the manner I have mentioned in another part of this report, I am confident we could have held the fort against all his assaults during the day, when, if we had been properly supported during the night by the major-general commanding at Memphis, a glorious victory to the Union cause would have been the result of the next day's operations.
>
> In conclusion, it may not be altogether improper to state that I was one of the number wounded, at first considered mortally, after the surrender; and but for the aid soon afterward extended to me by a Confederate captain, who was a member of an order to which I belong (Free Masonry), I would in all probability have shared the fate of many of my comrades who were murdered after having been wounded. This captain had me carried into a small shanty, where he gave me some brandy and water. He was soon ordered to his company, and I was carried by the rebels into the barracks which they had occupied during the most of the engagement. Here had been collected a great number of our wounded, some of whom had already died. Early the next morning these barracks were set on fire by order of a rebel officer, who had been informed that they contained Federal wounded. I was rendered entirely helpless from the nature of my wound, the ball having entered my right side, and ranging downward, grazed my lung, and deeply imbedded itself in my hip (where it still remains) out of easy reach of surgical instruments. In this condition I had almost given up every hope of being saved from a horrible death, when one of my own men, who was less severely wounded than myself, succeeded in drawing me out of the building, which the flames were then rapidly consuming.[93]

Lieutenant Leaming was carried on board the *Platte Valley* along with several score of wounded and taken to Mound City, Illinois, where he recovered. After being removed from the burning building, Lieutenant Leaming was assembled with others in a little gulley. He was lying a short distance from a wounded Negro "when a secesh soldier came up to him and said: 'What in hell are you doing here?' The colored soldier said he wanted to get on the gunboat. The secesh soldier said: 'You want to fight us again, do you? Damn you, I teach you,' and drew up his gun and shot him dead." Another black trooper, slightly wounded, was similarly approached by the same rebel, but the weapon misfired. A slight adjustment and the soldier was then killed. "I heard them shooting all around there—I suppose killing them."[94]

Other survivors gave testimony concerning the shooting of wounded the day after the battle. James Walls from Company E of the 13th Tennessee Cavalry told the investigating committee that while waiting for the boat to come up he saw "seceshs" order wounded blacks to "get up on their knees, when they would shoot them down like hogs."[95] Like Lieutenant Leaming, other troopers described being in buildings that were torched. Private Fulks claimed he was in the headquarters building when it was set afire but could not enlist the aid of a Confederate to help him out.[96] A civilian, John Penwell, asked an officer who ordered the burning of buildings "to let some of the men go in there, as there were some eight or more wounded men in there, and a negro who had a hip broken. He said 'The white men can help themselves out, the damned nigger shan't come out of that.'" He was able, with some effort to get himself out, but he did not know whether the others got out.[97] A member of Company B, 6th USHA saw Confederates place wounded in a building under the pretext a doctor would see them. Then the pine door was barred with a bolt, grass laid at the entrance and set afire.[98] Some witnesses reported seeing convalescents, perhaps as many as thirty, killed in a hospital building. Other wounded Union troops were observed killed in tents where they had gone for shelter. The bodies of smoldering troops were seen by many witnesses who came to the fort the following day. Several of these witnesses claimed they saw a few men nailed to buildings or logs that had been set afire.[99]

The fate of Major Bradford involved another tale of horror, that was singularly unique, if only because of the duration of his ordeal. According to Dr. Fitch, Major Bradford and Captain Posten came down the bluff with the retreating troops.

Major Bradford on reaching the edge of the River held up both hands, crying at the top of his voice that he surrendered, he had no coat, vest, or hat on, the Rebs fired volley after volley after volley at him. Bradford retreated backwards into the River, crying that he surrendered, until the water became so deep that he had to swim, he swam out some five or six rods into the River, and then turned and swam back to shore, during this time there were thousands of shots fired at him, after reaching the shore he started on the run up the bluff holding up his hands still crying that he surrendered, the Rebs fired at him until he passed up the bluff out of my sight.[100]

Bradford returned to shore after being hailed by a Confederate officer. Other officers standing nearby did not attempt to stop the shooting. According to two Federal officers who were not present on 12 April, Captain Theodore F. Bradford, signal officer for the gun boat and the Major's brother, was riddled with bullets on the order of General Forrest.[101]

Thomas Jordan and J. P. Pryor claim Bradford was paroled to bury his brother and then placed for the night in the custody of Colonel McCulloch. That evening while his host was asleep he supposedly slipped by careless sentinels and in disguise sought to make good his escape. Several days afterward he was recaptured and while enroute to Brownsville, after attempting to escape again, he was fatally shot. Dr. Wyeth, giving a slightly different version, wrote on the day after the battle that Bradford was recaptured near Covington and taken to Colonel Duckworth. Thereafter, he was marched with other prisoners to Brownsville, where General Chalmers was located. As they left Brownsville, Bradford was taken from the group and shot. Although Wyeth called this murder an "unwarrantable act," he agrees with Jordan the shooting was due "to private vengeance for well authenticated outrages committed by Bradford and his band upon the defenseless families of the men of Forrest's Cavalry."[102] Dr. Fitch reported seeing Major Bradford again at the fort at about 7:00 P.M. and thereafter heard, although he doubted the truth thereof, that Major Bradford had been paroled for twenty-four hours. W. R. McLagan, a recent Confederate conscript who escaped from Forrest's forces at Jackson with twenty-five others and eventually made his way to Memphis, related to the Congressional Committee events that appear reliable and unembellished by contrived rationalization. McLagan swore Bradford arrived at Covington underguard, sixteen miles from Fort Pillow on the evening of 12 April. On 13 April they completed a march to Brownsville where they stayed until 14 April.

Previous to our leaving Brownsville, five of the guards were ordered back to Duckworth's headquarters. Those five guards seemed to have received special instructions about something, I don't know what. After marching about five miles from Brownsville, we halted, that is, the two companies of the rebels. These five guards then took Major Bradford out about fifty yards from the road. He seemed to understand what they were going to do with him. He asked for mercy, and said that he had fought them manfully, and wished to be treated as a prisoner of war. Three of the five guards shot him. One shot struck him about in the temple; a second in the left breast, and the third shot went through the thick part of the thigh. He was killed instantly. They left his body lying there. I escaped from the rebels at Jackson. I left on the Friday morning about 2 o'clock and, Saturday night about 12 o'clock I came back where the murder was committed, and saw his body there, yet unburied. The moon was shining brightly, and it seemed to me that the buzzards had eaten his face considerably.

Question. Did you hear them give any reason for shooting Major Bradford?

Answer. Simply that he was a Tennessee traitor, and to them they showed no quarter. They said that he was a Tennessean, and had joined the Yankee army, and they showed them no quarter. I think myself that the order for shooting Major Bradford was given by Colonel Duckworth, for the reasons I have stated.

Question. What was the officer in command at the time he was shot?

Answer. A lieutenant went out with him. He was one of the five guards.

Question. Who commanded the two companies of rebels?

Answer. I do not know who ranked in these two companies. Russell and Lawler commanded the companies. Duckworth, who, I think gave the order for killing Major Bradford, belongs to Chalmer's command. He is a notorious scoundrel. He never had any reputation, either before the war or afterward.

Question. Did Major Bradford have on his uniform?

Answer: No, sir. He had tried to conceal his identity as much as possible, by putting on citizen's clothes, as he said that he had enemies among them, who would kill him if they knew him.[103]

Major Bradford justifiably feared for his life. His death was an intentional act of murder while he was a prisoner of war—an act that exceeded all bounds of decency and was without lawful authority or reason.

Captain Carl A. Lamberg, who was not present during the engagement, reported on the fate of a section of his battery, Battery D, 2nd U.S. Colored Light Artillery, which was sent to the fort on special assignment. Out of a complement of 1 commissioned officer and 34 enlisted men, Captain Lamberg reported 6 enlisted men killed, 4 wounded, 1 man escaped, 5 known prisoners, and 1 officer and 18 enlisted men missing, with no information about their fate. Relying on the information provided by one of his men who returned wounded to Memphis two days after the engagement, the captain wrote Private Kennedy saw five wounded members of the battery who were lying in their tents, after the surrender, killed by the rebels. A wounded black woman was also seen as she was shot through the head and killed. The company commander of the battery was last observed in the river with others who were being shot at by the rebels. Private Kennedy did not know the fate of Lieutenant Hunter because he was himself shot and dragged away at that moment.[104]

On 13 June 1864, General Forrest wrote Major General Washburn, who had replaced General Hurlbut as commanding officer of the 16th Corps at Memphis.[105] General Forrest expressed his concern

> that all negro troops stationed in Memphis took an oath on their knees, in the presence of Major-General Hurlbut and other officers of your army, to avenge Fort Pillow, and that they would show my troops no quarter. . . . The recent battle of Tishomingo Creek (Brices Cross Roads) was far more bloody than it would otherwise have been but for the fact that your men evidently expected to be slaughtered when captured, and both sides acted as though neither felt safe in surrendering, even when further resistence was useless.

Claiming that he had "conducted the war on civilized principles" he inquired whether his men in Federal hands would be treated as other Confederate prisoners and "the course intended to be pursued in regard to those who may hereafter fall into your hands."[106]

Thus began a series of correspondence that reflected the concerns between rival commanders in the West Tennessee theater of operations, the tenor of which suggests their sense of responsibility and attitude toward blacks in arms, as prisoners, and the Fort Pillow incident.

Major General Washburn, in a letter dated 17 June had written Major General S. D. Lee, Forrest's superior officer, regarding the treatment of black troops captured at Brice's Cross Roads. Rumors abounded at this latest encounter with Forrest's forces that the atrocities committed at Fort Pillow had been repeated at Brice's Cross Roads. General Washburn feared that "if true and not disavowed they must lead to consequences hereafter fearful to contemplate." In the expectation that the Confederate govern-

ment would disavow the action of the commanding general at
Fort Pillow, he refrained from issuing instructions with respect to
rebels taken prisoner by black troops, "but seeing no disavowal
on the part of the Confederate Government, but on the contrary
laudations from the entire Southern press of the perpetrators of
the massacre, I may safely presume that indiscriminate slaughter
is to be the fate of colored troops that fall into your hands." The
general then advised "If it is intended to raise the black flag
against that unfortunate race, they will cheerfully accept the issue.
Up to this time no troops have fought more gallantly and none
have conducted themselves with greater propriety. They have fully
vindicated their right (so long denied) to be treated as men."[107]

In response to the letter from General Forrest, General Washburn admitted that black troops at Memphis did take an oath to
avenge Fort Pillow, but it was solely "the result of their own sense
of what was due to themselves and their fellows, who had been
mercilessly slaughtered." Regarding any claim that the black
troops went into the field harboring a fear of being murdered,
General Washburn concluded, Fort Pillow justified that belief.
The general accepted with "satisfaction" Forrest's intimation that
the casualties at Brice's Cross Roads resulted rather "from the
desperation with which they fought than a predetermined intention to give them no quarter." General Washburn informed his
adversary "that the attempt to intimidate the colored troops by
indiscriminate slaughter had signally failed, and that instead of a
feeling of terror you have aroused a spirit of courage and desperation that will not down at your bidding."[108] In a circumlocutory
manner, General Washburn hinted at the possibility of retaliation
when he suggested that unless Forrest's command did something
that would exclude captured Confederates from being treated as
prisoners of war, they would be accorded the treatment a humane
government extends to its prisoners.

General Forrest was incensed by General Washburn's letters.
Excerpts of his written communications give undeniable insight
into the southern military's attitude regarding blacks under arms.
This attitude had its origin in racial fears that could not be assuaged. Only by violently lashing out at blacks could the Confederacy manifest their scorn for the Federal policy of mustering
blacks into the armed services of the North and contempt for the
idea that blacks could become something other than chattels.

Forrest wrote, "I regard your letter as discourteous to the commanding officer of this department, and grossly insulting to my-

self . . . denouncing me as a murderer and as guilty of the wholesale slaughter of the garrison at Fort Pillow." Without proffering any formal refutation, he said the charges were unfounded and unwarranted and officers should leave to their respective governments the question of whether black troops will be treated as prisoners of war and subject to exchange. He regarded "captured negroes as [he did] other captured property and not as captured soldiers." General Forrest proclaimed "it is not the policy nor the interest of the South to destroy the negro—on the contrary, to preserve and protect him—and all who have surrendered to us have received kind and humane treatment." General Forrest's sophism of 21 June is a study in literary legerdemain, in which he avoids the factual reality and consequences of Fort Pillow, and attempts instead to place the blame for waving the black flag policy of no quarter on northern authorities.

> In your letter you acknowledge the fact that the negro troops did take an oath on bended knee to show no quarter to my men; and you say further, "you have no doubt that they went to the battlefield expecting to be slaughtered," and admit also the probability of their having proclaimed on their march that no quarter would be shown us. Such being the case, why do you ask for the disavowal on the part of the commanding general of this department or the Government in regard to the loss of life at Tishomingo Creek? That your troops expected to be slaughtered, appears to me, after the oath they took, to be a very reasonable and natural expectation. Yet you, who sent them out, knowing and now admitting that they had sworn to such a policy, are complaining of atrocities, and demanding acknowledgments and disavowals on the part of the very men you went forth sworn to slay whenever in your power. I will in all candor and truth say to you that I had only heard these things, but did not believe them to be true; at any rate, to the extent of your admission; indeed, I did not attach to them the importance they deserved, nor did I know of the threatened vengeance, as proclaimed along their lines of march, until the contest was over. Had I and my men known it as you admit it, the battle of Tishomingo Creek would have been noted as the bloodiest battle of the war. That you sanctioned this policy is plain, for you to say now "that if the negro is treated as a prisoner of war you will receive with pleasure the announcement, and will explain the fact to your colored troops at once, and desire (not order) that they recall the oath; but if they are either to be slaughtered or returned to slavery let the oath stand."
>
> Your rank forbids a doubt as to the fact that you and every officer and man of your department is identified with this policy and responsible for it, and I shall not permit you, notwithstanding, by your stud-

ied language in both your communications, you seek to limit the operations of your unholy scheme and visit its terrible consequences alone upon that ignorant, deluded but unfortunate people, the negro, whose destruction you are planning in order to accomplish ours. The negroes have our sympathy, and so far as consistent with safety will spare them at the expense of those who are alone responsible for the inauguration of a worse than savage warfare.

It is not yet too late for you to retrace your steps and arrest the storm.[109]

Major General S. D. Lee shared General Forrest's sentiments and found Washburn's letter of 17 June equally offensive. Asserting that the Federals "assumed as correct an exaggerated statement of the circumstances . . . relying solely upon the evidence of those who would naturally give a distored history of the affair," General Lee continued:

The version given by you and your Government is untrue, and not sustained by the facts to the extent that you indicate. The garrison was summoned in the usual manner, and its commanding officer assumed the responsibility of refusing to surrender, after having been informed by General Forrest of his ability to take the fort, and of his fears as to what the result would be in case the demand was complied with. The assault was made under a heavy fire and with considerable loss to the attacking party. Your colors were never lowered, and your garrison never surrendered, but retreated from the fort to the cover of the gun-boat with arms in their hands, and constantly using them. This was true, particularly of your colored troops, who had been firmly convinced by your teachings of the certainty of their slaughter in case of capture. Even under these circumstances, many of your men, white and black, were taken prisoners.

"Fearful results" were expected to follow the refusal to surrender at Fort Pillow because the Federals "had a servile race, armed against their masters and in a country which had been desolated by almost unprecedented outrages."

Regarding the black troops engaged at Brice's Cross-Roads, he added, with sardonic flare

In their panic they acted as might have been expected from their previous impressions. I do not think many of them were killed. They are yet wandering over the country, attempting to return to their masters. With reference to the status of those captured at Tishomingo Creek and Fort Pillow, I will state that, unless otherwise ordered by my Government, they will not be regarded as prisoners of war, but will be retained and humanely treated, subject to such future instructions as may be indicated.[110]

General Lee then parried with the threat that if the black flag were raised, no distinction would be made between white and black troops.

General Washburn's response to General S. D. Lee paralleled additional comments he had dispatched to General Forrest dated 2 and 3 July.

In my last letter to General Forrest I stated that the treatment which Federal soldiers received would be their guide hereafter, and that if you give no quarter you need expect none. If you observe the rules of civilized warfare I shall rejoice at it, as no one can regret more than myself a resort to such measures as the laws of war justify toward an enemy that gives no quarter. Your remark that our colored soldiers "will not be regarded as prisoners of war, but will be retained and humanely treated," indicating that you consider them as of more worth and importance than your own soldiers who are now in our hands, is certainly very complimentary to our colored troops, though but a tardy acknowledgment of their bravery and devotion as soldiers; but such fair words can neither do justice to the colored soldiers who were butchered at Fort Pillow after they had surrendered to their victors, nor relieve yourself, General Forrest, and the troops serving under you from the fearful responsibility now resting upon you for those wanton and unparalleled barbarities. I concur in your remark that if the black flag is once raised there can be no distinction so far as our soldiers are concerned. No distinction in this regard as to color is known to the laws of war, and you may rest assured that the outrages we complain of are felt by our white soldiers, no less than by our black ones, as insults to their common banner, the flag of the United States.

I will close by a reference to your statement that many of our colored soldiers "are yet wandering over the country attempting to return to their master." If this remark is intended as a joke, it is acknowledged as a good one, but if stated as a fact, permit me to correct your misapprehensions by informing you that most of them have rejoined their respective commands, their search for their late "masters" having proved bootless; and I think I do not exaggerate in assuring you that there is not a colored soldier here who does not prefer the fate of his comrades at Fort Pillow to being returned to his "master."[111]

Concluding that further discussion would be useless, General Washburn observed that the record being established, let "a candid world judge of it."[112]

The colors of Forrest's organization were to have inscribed

therein the victories of Union City and Fort Pillow. President Jefferson Davis and Confederate Secretary J. A. Seddon approved the actions taken at Fort Pillow, and a resolution was adopted by the Congress of the Confederate States of America on 23 May 1864 expressing its appreciation for Forrest and his command's "brilliant" and "successful campaign" in Mississippi, West Tennessee, and Kentucky. In an initial dispatch from General Forrest dated 15 April 1864, he estimated that after storming the fort and a contest of thirty minutes he captured the entire garrison, killing five hundred, including all the officers, and obtained a large amount of stores together with two hundred horses. A second report of the same date, with measured hyperbole, described the scene after the assault.

> The victory was complete, and the loss of the enemy will never be known from the fact that large numbers ran into the river and were shot and drowned. The force was composed of about 500 negroes and 200 white soldiers [Tennessee Torries]. *THE RIVER WAS DYED WITH THE BLOOD OF THE SLAUGHTER FOR 200 YARDS.* There was in the fort a large number of citizens who had fled there to escape the conscript law. Most of these ran into the river and were drowned.
> The approximate loss was upward of 500 killed, but few of the officers escaping.
> *IT IS HOPED THAT THESE FACTS WILL DEMONSTRATE TO THE NORTHERN PEOPLE THAT NEGRO SOLDIERS CANNOT COPE WITH SOUTHERNERS.* We still hold the fort.[113]

A third report from Jackson, Tennessee, addressed to Jefferson Davis, acknowledged the "enemy attempted to retreat to the river, either for protection of gun-boats or to escape, and the slaughter was heavy. There were many Union men who had taken shelter in the fort also, many of whom in their fright leaped into the river and were drowned. It is safe to say that in troops, negroes and citizens the killed, wounded and drowned will range from 450 to 500."

He also expressed his gratification in being able to report the capture of Hawkins at Union City, Major Bradford at Fort Pillow, and the defeat of Colonel Hurst, which devastated the Tennessee Federal regiments in that part of the country. "Their acts of oppression, murder and plunder made them a terror to the whole land."[114]

It was not until 1 August that General Forrest's official report was found among General Polk's papers. The report was released for publication by the Confederate government to refute the slander generated by the northern press and Federal government against Forrest, who, according to Jefferson Davis, rather than demonstrating cruelty, "exhibited forbearance and clemency far exceeding the usage of war under like circumstances."[115] The report was written two weeks after the attack—26 April—during a time when the flames of public outrage were being fanned by the furious invective in the northern press and an official investigation had been announced by the Federal authorities.

General Forrest stated that after several hours of hard fighting in which admittedly he sustained "considerable loss," the "desired position was obtained." He described the Confederate line, as others had, as coming within one hundred yards of the fort and completely enveloping the fort from Coal Creek to the bluff of the Mississippi on the left. The report continued:

> . . . being confident of my ability to take the fort by assault, and desiring to prevent further loss of life, I sent, under flag of truce, a demand for the unconditional surrender of the garrison. . . . The gun-boat had ceased firing, but the smoke of three other boats ascending the river was in view, the foremost boat apparently crowded with troops, and believing the request for an hour was to gain time for re-enforcements to arrive, and that the desire to consult the officers of the gun-boat was a pretext by which they desired improperly to communicate with her.

Forrest sent the second communication giving the garrison twenty minutes to reply purportedly because of this perceived threat.

The report further stated that

> dispositions had all been made, and my forces were in a position that would enable me to take the fort with less loss than to have withdrawn under fire, and it seemed to me so perfectly apparent to the garrison that such was the case, that I deemed their capture without further bloodshed a certainty. After some little delay seeing a message delivered to Captain Goodman, I rode up myself to where the notes were received and delivered. The answer was handed me, written in pencil on a slip of paper, without envelope, and was, as well I remember in these words: "Negotiations will not attain the desired object." As the officers who were in charge of the Federal flag of truce had expressed a doubt as to my presence, and had pronounced the demand a trick, I handed them back the note saying: "I am General Forrest; go back and say to Major Booth that I demand answer in plain, unmistakable English. Will he fight or surrender?" Returning to my original position, before the expiration of twenty minutes I received a reply, . . . in which the garrison refused to surrender.

While these negotiations were pending the steamers from below were rapidly approaching the fort. The foremost was the Olive Branch, whose position and movements indicated her intention to land. A few shots fired into her caused her to leave the shore and make for the opposite. One other boat passed up on the far side of the river, the third one turned back.

The time having expired, I directed Brigadier-General Chalmers to prepare for the assault. Bell's brigade occupied the right, with his extreme right resting on Coal Creek. McCulloch's brigade occupied the left, extending from the center to the river. Three companies of his left regiment were placed in an old rifle-pit on the left and almost in the rear of the fort, which had evidently been thrown up for the protection of sharpshooters or riflemen in supporting the water batteries below. On the right a portion of Barteau's regiment, of Bell's brigade, was also under the bluff and in rear of the fort. I dispatched staff officers to Colonels Bell and McCulloch, commanding brigades, to say to them that I should watch with interest the conduct of the troops; that Missourians, Mississippians, and Tennesseeans surrounded the works, and I desired to see who would first scale the fort. Fearing the gun-boats and transports might attempt a landing, I directed my aide-de-camp, Capt. Charles W. Anderson, to assume command of the three companies on the left and rear of the fort and hold the position against anything that might come by land or water, but to take no part in the assault on the fort. Everything being ready, the bugle sounded the charge, which was made with a yell, and the works carried without a perceptible halt in any part of the line. As our troops mounted and poured into the fortification the enemy retreated toward the river, arms in hand and firing back, and their colors flying, no doubt expecting the gun-boat to shell us away from the bluff and protect them until they could be taken off or re-enforced. As they descended the bank an enfilading and deadly fire was poured into them by the troops under Captain Anderson, on the left, and Barteau's detachment on the right. Until this fire was opened upon them, at a distance varying from 30 to 100 yards, they were evidently ignorant of any force having gained their rear. The regiment who had stormed and carried the fort also poured a destructive fire into the rear of the retreating and now panic-stricken and almost decimated garrison. Fortunately for those of the enemy who survived this short but desperate struggle, some of our men cut the halyards, and the United States flag, floating from a tall mast in the center of the fort, came down. The forces stationed in the rear of the fort could see the flag, but were too far under the bluff to see the fort, and when the flag descended they ceased firing. But for this, so near were they to the enemy that few, if any, would have survived unhurt another volley. As it was, many rushed into the river and were drowned, and the actual loss of life will perhaps never be known, as there were quite a number of refugee citizens in the fort, many of whom were drowned and several killed in the retreat from the fort. In less than twenty minutes from the time the bugles sounded the charge firing had ceased and the work was done. One of the Parrott guns was turned on the gun-boat. She steamed off without replying. She had, as I afterward understood, expended all her ammunition, and was therefore powerless in affording the Federal garrison the aid and protection they doubtless expected of her when they retreated toward the river. Details were made, consisting of the captured Federals and negroes, in charge of their own officers, to collect together and bury the dead, which work continued until dark.[116]

After the engagement, Forrest directed his aide, Major Anderson, together with captured Federal officer Captain John T. Young, Provost Marshall and member of the fort's truce party, to make contact with the *New Era*. The purpose was to facilitate the removal of the seriously wounded. These efforts were without avail, and the gun boat sailed off out of harm's way. Captain Young was held as a prisoner of war after his capture at Fort Pillow. While detained at Cahaba, Alabama, he signed affidavits prepared for him by a southern judge. In the statement he claimed he "saw no ill-treatment of the wounded on the evening of the battle, or next morning." He claimed to have read Major Anderson's report, but could only confirm that "in regard to making disposition of Federal wounded left on the field at Fort Pillow" thought it correct. Nowhere in his statement is there any mention of facts concerning the massacre. Since Captain Young's statement was obtained under involuntary circumstances, the reliability of the document is highly suspect and without any value as to what occurred at the fort.[117]

General Forrest described his losses as 20 killed and 60 wounded. He estimated 228 Federals were buried on the evening of the battle and an undetermined number by details from the gun boats the following day. Of the 350 stand of small arms recovered, a few were acquired from within the fort while the majority were scattered from the brow of the hill to the water's edge, with many thrown into the water. Forrest's report calculated the number of captured Federals at 164 white and 75 black troops. He acknowledged capturing about 40 black women and children. In contrast, General Chalmers report of 7 May listed 164 white and only 40 black troops captured.

General Forrest's position respecting the charges made by the Federal government and the press concerning his and his command's conduct on that day in April 1864 may be best described in his own statement to Major General S. D. Lee on 24 June 1864. "As for myself, entirely conscious of right, I have no explanation, apologies, or disavowals to make to General Washburn, nor to any one else but my Government, through my superior officers."[118]

Describing the scene after all "negotiations for surrender proved unavailing," Major Anderson stated that within twenty minutes of the final assault "half the garrison lay weltering in their blood." The assaulting line having obtained the brow of the hill "mowed down the rear" while Barteau's detachment on the right and three companies on the left "poured into them an enfilading and deadly fire at a distance of 40 to 70 yards."

General James R. Chalmers, on addressing his troops on their successful campaign in West Tennessee, proclaimed with equal animus that they had "taught the mongrel garrison of blacks and renegades a lesson long to be remembered."[119]

3

Anxiety in the Public Mind

Lieutenant Commander T. Pattison, in charge of the Memphis Naval Station, ordered the *USS Silver Cloud* shortly after 5:00 P.M. on 12 April to proceed without delay to Fort Pillow and render whatever assistance was required.[1] The vessel was under the command of acting Master W. Ferguson. The *Silver Cloud,* her boilers partially disabled, made the trip lashed to the *Platte Valley.* By late evening she was able to make full steam but remained attached to her escort. Captain Ferguson arrived at Fulton, a thriving steamboat landing, at 6:00 A.M. on the 13th. He cast off from the *Platte Valley* and proceeded to the fort, three miles further up river. On route he shelled "suspicious places" along the way until he came opposite the fort. "All the buildings round the fort and the fort itself were on fire, and when I arrived abreast the fort several of our troops, some of them wounded came out from their hiding places. I landed and took them aboard and whilst doing so was fired upon by sharpshooters, but no person was injured. I then stood out in the river again and commenced to shell the hills. About this time some cavalry showed themselves on the hills with a flag of truce."[2] At approximately 9:00 P.M. a truce was agreed upon which was to last until 5:00 P.M. for the purpose of burying the dead and removing the wounded. The *New Era* landed at this time and put a party ashore. The wounded subsequently were placed on board the *Platte Valley* and another vessel, the hospital ship, *Red Rover.* In his official report, Ferguson acknowledged receiving a total of eighty-nine wounded. These included the sixty paroled by the Confederates through the negotiations of Major Anderson and twenty others he picked up along the banks. About one hundred and fifty Federals were buried by the several details sent ashore for that purpose. One of the civilians who went ashore was a journalist. While his description of the battle appeared exaggerated with respect to the number of troops engaged, he confirms the shelling of rebel squads who

U.S.S. Red Rover. **Courtesy of the U.S. Army Military History Institute.**

were applying torches to the buildings (commissary, barracks, huts, stables, and twelve private stores). He also reported "the rebels rendered us efficient aid, facilitating as much as possible getting the wounded on board transport." He praised the officers and men of the *Platte Valley* for the manner in which they attended to the wounded. Civilian staterooms were made available. Immediately proper sustenance was obtained for those able to eat and nourishing drinks provided to those otherwise too infirm. Ladies on board assisted in the work of alleviating as far as possible the sufferings of the wounded.

When the *Silver Cloud* commenced its cannonading, it could be heard at the Confederate encampment some seven or eight miles from Fort Pillow on the Brownsville Road. Major Anderson, along with an escort of ten men and captured Yankee Young, was dispatched back to the fort to make communication for the purpose of delivering the wounded. Anderson claims the first thing he did upon arriving at the fort was to cause all of General Chalmer's details to be withdrawn. Upon securing the truce on board the

Silver Cloud Anderson proceeded to notify Chalmers of the situation and invited Chalmers and his aides to join him. The fort was cleared of rebel stragglers, and initially the wounded were placed only aboard the *Platte Valley* so as to facilitate preparing a complete list of parolees.

Major Anderson permitted Captain Young to have the parole of the fort in order to visit with his wife who had come down on one of the steamers out of concern for his well being. Captain Young was looked upon with some suspicion because of the attention he received from the Confederates. "It was a subject of considerable remark that Captain Young was treated by the rebels with so much favor—and it is said that his brother, who has been in the rebel army, kept a grog shop at the fort and was a rebel sympathizer."[3] Most of the Federal prisoners were sent to the dreaded Andersonville prison which was substantially larger and not as well administrated as the Cahaba detention facility that housed Young.

"Permission was given to all the passengers on the three steamers to visit the fort, and all of them did so, many of them bringing back in their hands buckles, belts, balls, buttons, etc., picked up on the grounds, which they requested permission to carry with them as relics or mementos of Fort Pillow. All such requests were cheerfully and pleasantly granted." Near the hour of the truce expiration, the steamers departed while Captain Ferguson prepared to "let go his lines and depart at his leisure." Anderson "saluted him an adieu" and then proceeded up the bluff where the remaining buildings that had been "preserved for the accommodation of the Federal wounded" were torched.[4]

While the work of bringing the wounded down the bluffs for placement aboard the *Platte Valley* and burial details were in progress, several Union officers aboard the *Platte Valley* extended an invitation to General Chalmers and some of the other rebels present to come aboard. While on board "some of our officers showed them great deference, drinking with them and showing other marks of courtesy."[5] This scene of fraternization and sycophant between Confederate and Union officers was observed by other correspondents present and condemned as "toadyism." Quoting a correspondent from the *Missouri Democrat*, the *New York Times* reported the officers "made themselves conspicuous in fawning around the rebel officers. They brought General Chalmers on board the *Platte Valley*, drank with them, introduced them to their wives and invited them to dinner."[6]

Another journalist with the *Springfield Illinois State Journal* described General Chalmers as he appeared aboard the steamer "where some Union Officers were base enough to give him a hospitable welcome."

> General Chalmers came on board to drink at the bar, and seeing him closely, I discovered that "chivalry" consists in a handsome suit of gray, ornamented with silver stars and gracefully worn, a drab cavalier hat and long black plumes, with gay sash and glittering arms. This stylish looking villain raised his eyes as he passed me with as much courtier-like ease and grace as if he had been in a ballroom, and bowed until the plumes of the hat he held in his hand trailed on the floor. With a look that would have murdered him where he stood, if a look had power to kill, I met his glance. It was apparent to all that he was fully conscious his courtesy was resented as an insult, for he changed countenance, dropped his eyes and quietly passed on.
> At noon he came on board again, accompanied by his staff, and was invited to dine by some Union officers, passengers on the boat. I regret that I cannot give the names of these men who disgraced their uniforms so wantonly while our murdered men were lying bathed in blood before their eyes. These Union friends of their country's foes had rebel wives who received the illustrious butcher with cordiality and delight, and I heard Chalmers exclaim that it did him good "to shake hands, with thorough rebel ladies once more."[7]

The congressional investigators decried as shameful and astounding the fact that U.S. Army officers could "make themselves disgracefully conspicuous in bestowing civilities and attention upon rebel officers, even while they were boasting of the murders they had there committed." While the names of the "officers who have inflicted so foul a stain upon the honor of our army" were not then known to the committee, the committee was confident their identity would be ascertained and they would receive "the punishment they so richly merit."[8] Many years after the incident, Major Anderson recalled the invitation to have "a parting glass" with several lieutenants at the *Platte Valley* bar. "For this courtesy and kindness, one officer was cashiered and the other reduced to the ranks."[9]

Significantly, to the extent these journalists were able to interview survivors, one reporter at least confirmed the same accounts given subsequently to the congressional investigating committee by two participants and reported in Dr. Fitch's statement.[10] This reporter counted fifty dead strewn along the river bank. The journalist accounts depicted "indiscriminate butchery" in lurid detail after the rebels had possession of the fort and the survivors had surrendered. In many respects these dispatches were an appeal, not all too subtle, or devoid of partisan favoritism, to engender Union outrage and scorn.

No quarter was intended for them. The blacks and their officers were shot down, bayoneted and put to the sworn in cold blood—the helpless victims of the perfidy by which they were overpowered, and of the savage, barbarous, brutal, devilish blood-thirstiness that burned in the hearts and impelled the arm of their victors reveling in their fraudulently gotten victory.

Out of four hundred negro soldiers only about twenty survive! At least three hundred of them were destroyed after the surrender! This is the statement of the rebel General Chalmers himself to our informant. Negroes were compelled to dig trenches into which they were thrown alive! Our informant—an officer in whose probity and moderation we have entire confidence—says he saw the charred remains of negro soldiers mingled with the ashes of their tents. Their tents were fired, and they were prevented from escaping.

They were deliberately burned to death! The spectacle, as presented to the eyes of our informant, was one that no human being, and no inhabitant of perdition, imagined within the range of human or inhuman possibilities on the face of the earth. The wounded, with great gashes in the head, and with limbs dissevered from the body, writhed and yelled with agony that terrified the horses, but made the rebel fiends in human shape laugh, and jest, and jeer.[11]

Enraged by the stubborn resistance offered to them by its heroic defenders, when they were enabled to seize it at last by overwhelming numbers, they fell upon the victims without mercy or quarter. Our brave troops, white and black, were put to death in cold blood, tender women and little children were bayoneted; neither age nor sex were a protection against the bloodthirsty fury of these savages and out of a noble garrison of six hundred men scarcely one-third remain alive.[12]

A dispatch from Cairo dated 14 April reported "Immediately upon the surrender ensued a scene which utterly baffles description. Up to that time, comparatively few of our men had been killed; but, insatiate as fiends, bloodthirsty as devils incarnate, the Confederates commenced an indiscriminate butchery of the whites and blacks, including those of both colors who had been previously wounded."[13]

These descriptions caused outrage among the public and lead to a call for retaliation to be sanctioned by the Federal government. Contrary to Forrest's assessment that the battle's outcome would teach the North that black troops were no match for their southern opponents, the opposite occurred. The effect was to arouse wrath from the pulpit, press, and the public. The incident fed into the hands of abolitionists whose cause would find additional grist. Racial prejudice that initially created skepticism among white troops in the efficacy of arming blacks, and had been slowly dissipating through combat, now was further eroded by the fate of their comrades in arms. Up to this juncture in the war, the South's fears were unrealized as black men in arms adhered to the rules of war. The *New York Evening Post* stated the principle clearly.

> [I]f the rebels adopt the practice of refusing to give quarter to troops who have surrendered, after a summons to surrender has been declined, our troops should be instructed to do the same. If they authorize men wearing their uniform to commit obscene and horrible outrages upon non-combatants or upon the bodies of the dead, we should authorize our soldiers to shoot them down, wherever they are met, like so many dogs. . . .
>
> It seems to us that public opinion, the interests of civilization, good faith and expediency all require that in every instance in which our troops are made slaves some rebel officer should be set to work at hard labor. A little experience in the trenches, or on the public roads, would cure these dainty, aristocratic gentlemen of their fondness for using other people's muscles. . . .
>
> But something is expected of the government, and we think it could be nothing better than establish the rule we have just suggested.[14]

These remonstrations for retaliation found equal voice among the military.

Lieutenant Leaming expressed the belief in regard to the "outrages perpetrated by the rebels that some sort of retaliation should be adopted as the surest method of preventing a recurrence of the fiendish barbarities practiced on the defenders of our flag at Fort Pillow."[15] General Hurlbut called attention to the War Department for the "necessity of some vigorous action on their part to insure the treatment due to soldiers to our colored troops. Not only is it due our good name, but it will be necessary to preserve discipline among them. In case of an action in which they shall be successfully engaged, it will be nearly impracticable to restrain them from retaliation."[16] Writing from Memphis, General Chetlain described the Fort Pillow affair as "the most infernal outrage that has been committed since the war began." He described the excitement among the black troops under his command and postured "If this is to be the game of the enemy they will soon learn that it is one at which two can play." Like others, he concluded, "I feel that the blood of these heroes must be avenged."[17]

The Christian Reporter editorialized that the disaster at Fort Pillow may have been inspired by the government's duplicitous policy toward black soldiers. True, unequal pay, a cadre of white only officers, at times inferior equipment, and in the main relegation to garrison or fatigue duties did not conjure an impression of confidence.[18] *The Christian Reporter* emphasized

> that the massacre, at Fort Pillow, has been invited by the tardiness of the government, and the action of Congress. While they have professed to regard every man wearing the U.S. uniform, as being equal in theory, they have acted towards the black soldiers, in such a way, as to convince the Confederate government that they, themselves, do not regard the black soldiers as equal to the white. The rebels have taken advantage of this equivocation, to commit just such horrible butchery as that at Fort Pillow.[19]

Chagrined over the "desperate and reckless wretches like this blackleg Forrest" the *New York Evening Post*[20] also found fault with the government.

> But let us tell our military authorities and members of Congress that if they would have the rebels treat our black troops as soldiers, they must themselves begin by treating them as such. While they refuse to pay them the same bounties and rates that they pay white soldiers, whose services are not a whit more efficient, they virtually treat them as an inferior class, and to that extent justify the outrages committed by the rebel assassins.

On the same day the *Evening Post* editorial appeared, President Lincoln spoke before a large crowd at the Baltimore Sanitary Fair. He applauded the open Union sympathies in the city which had not been prevalent three years previously. In expressing the disappointment of many, however, that no one expected the war to have lasted as long, he pondered "so true is it that man proposes and God disposes." He then expounded on how the meaning of liberty may be defined by different expectations. For some liberty is to do as one pleases with himself as well as with the product of one's labor; while others believe liberty means they can do as they please with other men and other men's labor. Before concluding his remarks he felt constrained to speak of a "painful rumor" regarding the events at Fort Pillow.

"There seems to be some anxiety in the public mind," he stated,

whether the government is doing its duty to the colored soldier, and to the service, at this point. At the beginning of the war, and for some time, the use of colored troops was not contemplated; and how the change of purpose was wrought I will not now take time to explain. Upon a clear conviction of duty, I resolved to turn that element of strength to account; and I am responsible for it to the American people, to the Christian world, to history and in my final account to God. Having determined to use the negro as a soldier, there is no way but to give him all the protection given any other soldier. The difficulty is not in stating the principle, but in practically applying it. It is a mistake to suppose the government is indifferent to this matter, or is not doing the best it can in regard to it. We do not today know that a colored soldier, or white soldier commanding colored soldiers, has been massacred by the rebels when made a prisoner. We fear it,— believe it, I may say,—but we do not know it. To take the life of one of their prisoners on the assumption that they murder ours, when it is short of certainty that they do murder ours, might be too serious, too cruel, a mistake. We are having the Fort Pillow affair thoroughly investigated; and such investigation will probably show conclusively how the truth is. If after all that has been said it shall turn out that there has been no massacre at Fort Pillow, it will be almost safe to say there has been none, and will be none elsewhere. If there has been the massacre of three hundred there, or even the tenth part of three hundred, it will be conclusively proved; and being so proved, the retribution shall as surely come.[21]

Two weeks following this address President Lincoln gathered his cabinet for their advice. "It is now quite certain that a large number of our colored soldiers, with their white officers, were, by the rebel force, massacred after they had surrendered, at the recent capture of Fort Pillow. So much is known though the evidence is not yet quite ready to be laid before me. Meanwhile I will thank you to prepare, and give me in writing your opinion as to what course, the government should take in the case."[22]

Secretary of State Seward wanted to set aside numbers of prisoners in close confinement until the Confederate government gave satisfactory explanation or disavowed the incident or gave assurance against repetition. Chase, secretary of the treasury, agreed to the extent that the prisoners chosen should be from the highest rank. Secretary of the Army Stanton acquiesced but would deny Forrest and his command the benefit of amnesty or parole. Stanton would, in effect, have declared Forrest an outlaw if the Confederate government refused the demand to have him turned over to the Federal government. Secretary of the Navy Welles was in agreement with this proposition. Postmaster General Blair argued retaliation would not be civilized. He was inclined to pursue the actual offenders separately and when captured punish them summarily. He reasoned a proclamation to this effect would cause greater terror than punishing those not involved in the crime. Attorney General Bates of Missouri would not be party to any "cartel of blood and murder" and opined retaliation is not justice but "avowedly revenge." Usher from Indiana, secretary of the interior, agreed with Blair and Bates in condemning retaliation but believed it inexpedient to take some private action before the results of the pending great battles were known.[23]

"In the storm of guns and blood and death soon to be let loose by Grant and Sherman against Lee and Johnson, in the reddening streams and the shouting and crying with black silence after, and then the renewal of crimson explosions and the gray monotonous weariness—in this terrific grapple of guns and living wills and dying testaments the Fort Pillow affair was to sink to a lesser significance."[24] Indeed, with the ebbing rhetoric and the focusing of attention on emerging new offensives, Lincoln was not disposed to deflect the war effort for some personal adventure that would have no meaningful impact upon the conflict's duration or outcome.

4

An Unavoidable Loss

The battle of Fort Pillow was a tragic event whose consequences need not have occurred. The loss of the fort and the losses to the garrison were inevitable, although for different reasons. Considering the physical infirmities inherent in the fort's defenses, together with the cumulative impact of errant human judgment, the garrison was destined to fail in the face of a determined and creative assault. Too many factors of omission and commission were operating without any considered thought for the fate of a garrison that would be caught like an insect within the leaves of a Venus's-flytrap. Once the engagement commenced General Forrest well knew his quarry's fate was a certainty.

When General Forrest arrived on the field there were between nineteen hundred to possibly two thousand men comprising all the Confederate forces. Not all these troops would become participants in the engagement. Perhaps as many as every fourth man was detailed to holding horses. This then left an effective fighting force of about fifteen hundred.[1]

The initial dawn attack and capture of all but one or two of the pickets manning the outposts at the outer fortification was not a significant event. The Federal withdrawal from the second entrenchment or earthwork presented the more serious dilemma. Although the reason for recalling the men from these positions is unclear, it would appear from Lieutenant Leaming and the account of others that at least two assaults had been repulsed while these positions were occupied by the Federals. The testimony indicates that once Forrest's men gained these positions they were as well protected as the defenders esconced behind the most inner fortification. Major Anderson observed the Federals "were unable to depress their artillery so as to rake these slopes with grape and canister, and so far as safety was concerned, we were as well fortified as they were; the only difference was that they were on one side and we on the other of the same fortifica-

Confederate sharpshooters picking off Federal defenders at Fort Pillow. Courtesy of the Library of Congress.

tion."[2] The abandonment of this middle redoubt was perhaps the "key to the position, as it commanded the two ravines which nearly surrounded the fort, and could not have been occupied by the Confederates had this middle defense been held."[3] Forrest knew, with his troops in these ravines he had "the garrison at his mercy." This lapse of strategy was compounded by the additional withdrawal of troops from the rifle pits. The "unerring fire" of Confederate sharpshooters taking their aim from commanding knolls southeast of the fort enabled the most advanced Confederate troops to seek the shelter of these ravines. Their movements were fairly immune from harassment by the Federals, who for the most part were kept pinned down behind the main fortification. Anderson reported "they had no sharpshooters with which to annoy our main force, while ours sent a score of bullets at every head that appeared above the walls."[4] The Confederate sharpshooters, on the other hand, took advantage of the terrain some three hundred yards to the front and south of the fort. Owing to the peculiar, glacially formed profile the area was characterized by several high knolls affording the sharpshooters a clear field of fire to the top of the parapet and on line with the embrasures. On the other

UNION FORT
IDEALIZED PROFILE
SOUTH END

Profile, south end of Fort Pillow. Appeared in *Archaeological Investigations at Fort Pillow State Historic Area, 1976–1978.*

hand, the limited field of fire provided by the gun ports and the thickness of the parapet's walls precluded the Federals from positioning their weaponry to effectively fire other than over these abutting ravines and beyond the middle entrenchment. The space between each gun port and the gun port's width precluded over- lapping fire and created blind spots for the artillerists. The ri- flemen within the fort had their line of sight restricted by the breadth of the parapet, thereby creating a similar problem. A rifleman taking aim from within could only deflect the angle of his shot to a point no closer than many yards from the base of the outside parapet walls. In order to decrease this angle and cover the area directly in front of the base a rifleman would have to stand or kneel astride the top of the wall, completely exposing himself to Confederate sharpshooters. Some defenders were con- vinced that had the garrison not abandoned the middle trenches as well as the rifle pits the defenders would have been in a better defensive posture. The loss of these positions significantly contrib- uted to the garrison's defeat.

The mischief in this error of military strategy was made even more extreme by the existence of the barracks to the south of the fort. Major Booth realized too late and succeeded in only partially destroying the closest of these buildings during the initial engage- ment. Perhaps maintaining possession of the southern rifle pits

Southwest exterior of Fort Pillow parapet.

would have at least neutralized the efficacy of the rebels using the remaining buildings as cover to pour fire into the fort proper at relatively close range. Lieutenant Leaming described the shooting from these protected positions as "murderous" upon the men of the garrison and agreed the artillery could not be sufficiently depressed to render the barracks "untenable to the enemy."[5]

A serious dispute between the survivors and attacking forces focused around the deployment of Confederate troops during the period of time the flag of truce was in effect. This controversy has survived to this day as the focal point of much discourse between General Forrest's detractors, biographical admirers, and historians.

"During this cessation of firing on both sides, in consequence of the flag of truce offered by the enemy, and while the attention of both officers and men were naturally directed to the south side of the fort where the communications were being received and answered, Forrest had resorted to means the most foul and infamous ever adopted in the most barbarous ages of the world for the accomplishment of his design." He moved his troops under cover of a ravine and thick underbrush "into the very position he had been fighting to obtain throughout the entire engagement."[6]

This "gross violation of the rules of civilized warrfare," an accusation previously leveled against Forrest at Paducah and Columbus, was observed by many officers and men of the garrison. Lieutenant Van Horn reported the rebels were "crawling" up to the fort. Some enlisted men were even able to converse with the rebels as the latter bettered their positions. The rebels justified their movement under the conviction of "knowing their business."

Concedely some troops were moved to positions that were already in the possession of the Confederates. To the south, Forrest admits sending two hundred troops under the command of Major Anderson in order to prevent a disembarkation of Federals approaching from the river. A similar number from Barteau's regiment took a corresponding position below the bluff near the mouth of Cold Creek.[7] For those defending Forrest's actions, this was a "clearly legitimate movement"[8] to minimize and deter the river borne threat. Along the Cold Creek ravine troops were deployed in positions already held by Colonel Bell for four hours. Historians are fairly in agreement that these violations of generally accepted standards of war did not alter the outcome of the battle. The encroachments, however, most assuredly facilitated the Federal defeat and contributed to the slaughter that occurred along the river embankment after the fort's defenses had been breached and the garrison's resistence overcome.

As a consequence of these movements Bell's brigade on the right, in position from thirty to one hundred feet of the ditch, and McCulloch's men, occupying the cabins to the left and facing the fort at a distance of sixty yards, were effectively reinforced. It will be remembered Forrest acknowledged that attainment of the desired positions, prior to his calling for the capitulation of the garrison, was not accomplished without considerable loss. The point then can fairly be made, had Forrest not moved up reinforcements during the cessation of fighting occasioned by the flag of truce, his casualties would have been higher and the assailment of the last redoubt would conceivably have been delayed until sufficient forces filled the ditch. Undoubtedly Forrest would never have attempted this final assault in a piecemeal fashion with less forces than he considered sufficient to accomplish the mission. These troops then not only supported those who already were in place for two hours but provided additional covering fire to assure this aspect of the assault's success.[9]

According to one studied analysis, the "most that can be charged against Forrest is that he violated the cease-fire by stationing Anderson's and Barteau's detachments along the river

Confederates storming Fort Pillow. Courtesy of the Library of Congress.

bank. But even here, it can be reasonably argued that he was justified in believing that the approaching steamships intended to aid the garrison and, therefore, in taking measures to forestall this action." Albert Castel concludes, "that the weight of the evidence and logic supports the Southern point of view . . . that the fort fell before the superior strength and strategy of Forrest, not as the result of a devious ruse."[10] Superior strength and strategy, however, were augmented by whatever number of additional troops Forrest permitted, without fear of molestation, to advance positions unrelated to the perceived river threat. Certainly, these Confederates were not redeployed during the truce solely as a deterrent to the approaching river vessels. Although the question may be rhetorical, once the steamer transporting Federal troops had passed, why did Forrest not withdraw the four hundred troops he placed to oppose this now nonexistent threat.

The fortunes of war obviously do not permit the refinements of play customarily followed in organized sports. Though a fighter, "Forrest was not accustomed to sacrifice men needlessly. He got results, but he wanted them as cheaply as possible."[11] Working men forward through the underbrush and stumps without the need for sharpshooter covering fire during the truce was more expedient. Whether in the first instance, the river vessels actually posed a realistic threat rather than a remote possibility, is also subject to serious question. As indicated earlier, Forrest, believing that the request for an hour delay by the garrison was a stalling tactic to receive reinforcements from the approaching steamers, issued the deployment orders to Anderson and Barteau. Several documents cast grave doubt regarding the river threat. In the log of the *New Era*, Acting Master Marshall wrote that at 9:30 A.M. the *Liberty* passed, landing at the coal barge which contained civilians and noncombatants he had previously towed out of danger above Cold Creek. Taking on board all those wishing to leave she proceeded down river, but not without taking a volley from the shore when passing the fort.[12]

At this same time General George F. Shepley was several miles below Fulton proceeding north in the *Olive Branch* when he was hailed from the shore that the fort was under attack. General Shepley was the former military governor of Louisiana who had been relieved from duty and directed to report to the commanding general of the army. He left New Orleans aboard the *Olive Branch* on the evening of 6 April. The *Olive Branch* was a private vessel not in the service of the government and carrying a large number of civilians. At Vicksburg, the steamer took on a portion of men from two batteries. In all there were about 120 men, with full compliment of horses, guns, caissons, wagons, field equipment, and presumably shells and powder. The troops were not carrying small arms. General Shepley ordered the captain of the *Olive Branch* not to turn around. He then directed some of the troops to board another vessel he had ordered alongside together with a section of battery when a "steamer with troops hove in sight." This steamer was the *Liberty*, and as she approached he saw U.S. Infantry aboard. She kept on going rapidly down with the current, only hailing the *Olive Branch*: "All right up there; you can go by, the gun boat is lying off the fort." General Shepley did not inquire further or order the *Liberty* alongside so as to determine what action the combined forces he now had at his disposal could be put for purposes of investigating the situation and bringing aid to the garrison. The time of this encounter must have been between noon and 1:00 P.M., since Shepley, after getting underway, was above the fort when the Confederate flag was raised—between 3:30 and 4:00 P.M.

The *Olive Branch* proceeded up river, and as it neared the fort, she received musketry fire from the shore aimed at the pilot house. The steamer continued to report to the gunboat on station. One of the two steamers trailing the *Olive Branch* put about and headed down river while the other passed up the far side of the river.

An officer from the *New Era* approached in a small boat and "said he did not want any boat to stop" and that the *Olive Branch* should proceed to Cairo and have them send him four hundred rounds of ammunition. General Shelpley believed the object of the attack was to capture a river boat and not the fort. A flag of truce was flying, as was the U.S. flag, and no firing was heard. Since there was no communication from the fort, no attack in progress, and the *Liberty*'s message and the communication from the *New Era* did not auger any peril, he felt constrained to proceed up river. Since the *Olive Branch* was defenseless and carrying civilians, and the artillery pieces were incapable of attaining sufficient elevation to fire above the bluff, he could not have ordered effective assistance from the boat. At this same time, Forrest, who was waiting for a reply to his last communication for surrender, remarked to a member of his truce team, Captain Goodman, "She won't land."[13]

Forrest's biographer Wyeth claims that during the flag of truce a steamer was descending the river from above the fort.[14] Believing reinforcements were approaching, the general issued deployment orders to Captain Anderson and a portion of Barteau's regiment. Since the *Liberty*, the only boat descending the river, passed between 10:00 A.M. and 11:00 A.M., she could not have been a threat at about 3:00 P.M. when Forrest issued his orders. Charles Robinson, a civilian photographer who participated in the fight with Company C of the 13th Tennessee Cavalry, wrote to his parents on 17 April from Columbus, Kentucky. He recalled the "commander came around and said, '[y]ou have done well my boys. Hold out a little longer for there is a boat coming with reinforcements and if we can hold the place a little longer we will have plenty of help as there is a thousand soldiers on the boat.' I shall never forget the glad shout that went up from the little fort on this an[n]ouncement, nor will I forget how sad we all felt when the boat passed but never offered to land." Since this incident occurred "four hours" after the men had been fighting, the steamboat approaching from above could only have been the *Liberty* which passed well before 3:00 P.M.[15]

Wyeth additionally claimed no signal was ever made by the fort or gun boat for the *Olive Branch* "not to approach"[16] or, as observed by Henry, "to turn back or stand away toward the Arkansas shore."[17] The simple truth is that while no signal was made from the fort, the *Olive Branch* had no intention and made no effort to land but honored the truce flag and instructions from the captain of the *New Era*. While some apprehension was justified and taking precautions warranted, Barteau's movements placed his troops between two hundred fifty and three hundred yards from the only point where a landing could take place and clearly out of position to render effective fire against such a landing. The steamboat dock was near the southern ravine and below the rifle pits on that side of the bluff and not in clear sight from Barteau's position. A small detachment of less than the two hundred men Major Anderson had could effectively have dissuaded any attempt to disgorge in an orderly manner the cumbersome equipment of the artillery batteries, a fact no doubt appreciated by General Shepley and his aide, Captain Thornton. Forrest knew the *Olive Branch* would not land because, among several considerations, he too realized there was no position below the bluff to effectively place the artillery and no way to safely transport them up into the fort under fire.

When the *Olive Branch* was passing the fort, she did not return the musketry fire from the shore but proceeded to the *New Era* which was stationed slightly above the fort. At this juncture, any possible threat of a landing had passed and yet the precautionary detachments were not recalled during the fifteen to twenty minutes that must have elapsed before the final assault was made. As the *Olive Branch* proceeded beyond the fort the fighting was resumed and those on board heard the cacophony of battle and, after a few minutes, observed the rebel flag hoisted.

The violation of the flag of truce was not only in obtaining some positions previously unoccupied by the Confederates but in reinforcing and strengthening the positions they held and, more particularly, in accomplishing the real objective of sealing the fate of the garrison through the deployment of Anderson's and Barteau's men. The apprehension of water borne troops reinforcing the garrison was an exaggeration without basis and designed to give justification to troop movements during the truce period.

Whether General Shepley could have rendered effective aid while passing the fort is moot, since the truce effectively barred him from any landing. His error was not signaling the *Liberty* to hove to shore when the boats were several miles below the fort. In this manner, he could have conducted a reconnaissance in force from Fulton and possibly, positioned the batteries with supporting infantry to have rendered some aid from below the fort. Acting Master James Marshall of the *New Era*, gun boat No. 7, claimed he fired 285 rounds of shell, shrapnel, and canister; 375 rounds of rifle fire; and 96 rounds of revolver cartridges.[18] Contrary to some reports he was not out of ammunition but had 75 rounds left when the truce went into effect. In his official report he claimed at about fifteen minutes past noon the *New Era* began taking fire from two light artillery pieces under cover of Wolf's Hill as well as sharpshooters "firing on us from all directions."[19] In fact, while the gun boat was opposite the lower ravine, it had to close its ports and use small arms because of the heavy fire of musketry from the bluff according to civilian witness Elvis Bevel.[20]

Owing to the nature of the terrain around the fort, as well as trying to hit unseen targets by signal direction, accuracy was made extremely difficult. Testimony previously referred to by General Forrest and Lieutenant Leaming clearly indicate the *New Era*'s participation in the battle was wholly without effect. Perhaps the only salutory aspect of its presence was that the *New Era* early in the engagement, did successfully remove noncombatants and others attached to the fort who most certainly would have met a fate similar to that of their comrades had they not been taken off. All too much reliance was placed on the *New Era* for contributing to the defense of the fort. As a result of wind and current the *New Era* could not bring to bear more than the three 24 pounders mounted on her starboard side during any salvo. In addition, as she passed below the fort to fire in the ravine, musketry from the shore as well as shells from two light Confederate field pieces interfered with the cannoneers accuracy, and as a consequence most of her participation occurred above the fort near Cold Creek. Captain Marshall claimed right after the final assault that the rebels turned the guns of the fort on him and a Parrott shot went over the *New Era*. His justification for not being able to render assistance at this time was the fear his vessel would be captured or sunk were he to come downstream. Additionally, he dared not fire into the fort for fear of hitting remnants of the garrison. His testimony suggested "Had I been below here [Fort Pillow] at the time, I think I could have routed them out."[21] Captain Marshall's boastful assessment leaves open the question why he did not steam to the more advantageous position below during the truce except if, at it appears, the concern for his own safety and that of the boat dictated the extent of his valor. Suffice it to say, at a critical moment the gunboat was out of position and the captain exhibited a recreance that some would describe as "criminal prudence."[22]

The loss of the post may also be attributed to the quality of leadership and poor judgment displayed by several commanding officers. Major Booth, a native of Pennsylvania, was a regular army enlistee who attained the rank of quartermaster sergeant with the First Missouri Light Artillery prior to being accepted as a volunteer officer in the First Battalion, Sixth USCHA. General Hurlbut recommended him highly. Lieutenant Colonel Thomas H. Harris referred to Booth as "an officer of experience and tried courage, and irreproachable character."[23] Major Booth's inopportune awareness of some of the fort's weaknesses and an overconfidence in the garrison's defensive posture, despite his military and leadership qualities, were fatal strategy flaws. While the advantage the Confederates had in occupying the buildings and the inability to depress the artillery have been explained, Major Booth's reliance on his men and the fort's defenses also clouded his judgment when it came to digesting intelligence.

Captain Thomas P. Gray of the 7th Tennessee Cavalry reported to Major Booth on 30 March. The captain had escaped from his Confederate captors several days after his commanding officer, Colonel Hawkins, surrendered the entire Union City garrison to Colonel Duckworth of Forrest's command. Captain Gray indicated that on making his way to the fort the rumor along the road was that the rebels would attack Fort Pillow, although he thought otherwise because there was nothing occurring on the road to indicate anything more definite. Shortly after this information was received by Major Booth, perhaps nine or ten days later, a male courier with General Forrest, who traveled under the disguise of a woman for the purpose of procuring ordnance and ammunition in Federal held territory, was captured and brought to the fort. Lieutenant Rawley was known by the sobriquet of "Mollie." He testified at an investigation into secret societies that operated as fifth columnists and who were rumored to be comprised of Federal soldiers with southern sympathies. Lieutenant Rawley stated that while at Fort Pillow, a man who was familiar with the lieutenant's identity "said Forrest was coming with 4,000 men to take the place and he was going to take it if it took every man he had."[24] He told Major Booth what he had heard and expressed the opinion Forrest would take the place if he made the attempt. "My advice was to evacuate the fort or re-enforce it at once, for if Forrest did get possession the Federal forces, and especially the officers, would be badly used."[25] Lieutenant Rawley was transported to Memphis two days preceding the assault. Surely Booth could have requested reinforcements or at least sent scouts out to ascertain the reliability of the threat and the extent of Forrest's forces.

The lack of internal security within outposts such as Fort Pillow

was flagrant and notorious. The same evening "Mollie" left the
fort for Memphis the man who had advised him of Forrest's impending attack was permitted leave of the fort. While Lieutenant
Rawley was at headquarters this informant came in, and with a
Tennessee soldier attesting to his loyalty, Major Booth issued the
man a pass. Dr. Wyeth wrote "The Confederates were fortunate
in securing as a guide Mr. W. J. Shaw, a citizen of this vicinity,
who had recently been arrested by Major Bradford and confined
within the limits of the fort. Having escaped on the 11th, he was
entirely familiar with the topography of the enclosure, as well as
the number of troops defending the works."[26] In fact, it was more
than likely the fort contained at any time a number of southern
sympathizers. "Mollie" described in his testimony of having had
a conversation with a Mr. John Beauvais. Mr. Beauvais was a mer-
chant at the fort and under house arrest for selling munitions to
the Confederates, though on the eve of the battle he continued
to sell his nonmilitary wares.[27] This glimpse of loose martial control was consistent with the fear of some commanders that the
small posts along the river of no military importance or necessity
were "dens for the smugglers, contraband dealers and convenient
for supplying the guerrillas" in an abundance more valuable than
under their own occupation.[28] In writing to General Grant, General Sherman observed "All these stations are a weakness, and
offer tempting chances for plunder."[29]

To General Halleck, Sherman wrote the efforts to cover trading
schemes and local interests penalizes large armies by dividing
them into small units susceptible to surprise and capture. "The
recent garrison of Pillow was not a part of our army, but a nonde-
script body, in process of formation and posted there to cover a
trading port for the convenience of families supposed to be
friendly to us, or at least not hostile."[30] As if sealing the perverbial
barn door, on 20 April, General McPherson ordered the evacuation of weak points along the river. "The system of small isolated
posts is a bad one. They add very little to the safety of navigation
on the river or the security of the country, and are liable to be
surprised and captured."[31]

The vulnerability of posts like Fort Pillow, because of their
smaller garrisons and inadequate security, was apparent. The failure of commanding officers to appreciate these weaknesses only
encouraged the disaster that occurred. General Hurlbut, knowing
the command of the fort could devolve upon Major Bradford, a
very young man and "entirely inexperienced in these matters,"
conceded in his testimony before the congressional investigating

committee that the death of Major Booth, for whom he had "great confidence," "no doubt . . . was the immediate cause of the capture of the place."[32]

General Sherman was shocked at learning of the disaster because he believed the entire garrison together with its guns had been removed, as the fort was evacuated before the start of his Meridian campaign. He wired General Grant "I don't know what these men were doing at Fort Pillow. I ordered it to be abandoned before I went to Meridian, and it was so abandoned."[33] General Hurlbut, a man of contradiction and indecisiveness, gave conflicting testimony regarding the reoccupation of the site. He acknowledged that the fort was only "temporarily abandoned" until the 13th Tennessee could come down to occupy the place as a recruiting point. Owing, however, to the nature of the fortification, he did not want it to fall into rebel hands and thereby disrupt the passing of supplies and troops along the river. This concern for "uninterrupted communication by the river" obviously was not an enigma for General Sherman who voiced no concern about regarrisoning the site at the conclusion of the Meridian campaign. Neither was Sherman ever consulted by Hurlbut on the matter.

Following the Meridian campaign, General Sherman complained the expedition achieved minimal success and in some aspects was a complete failure. He attributed the failure to General William Sooy Smith, who instead of leaving Memphis on 1 February as ordered, delayed his departure until 11 February, thereby permitting Forrest to get the advantage and defeat Smith at Okolona. Smith, however, was not idle during this period. Having recently been put in charge of all the cavalry in the Department of Tennessee, on 1 February he ordered Major Bradford to continue his recruitment efforts from Fort Pillow. The major was to subsist off the countryside and attack guerrilla parties.[34] Hurlbut's primary intention was the enlistment of new troops from the area, and the defense of the river was an exaggerated anxiety that could not have been assuaged with the presence of inexperienced troops under the command of one in whom General Hurlbut lacked confidence.

Lieutenant Colonel Thomas H. Harris, testifying before the investigating committee at Memphis on 26 April, stated emphatically that the fort was occupied as a recruiting station rather than for any other purpose.[35]

General Hurlbut's incompetence was a signal flaw. This could not have been more grossly displayed than through the delivery of unclear and imprecise instructions to a man whose military background was limited and untried. On 28 March, he communicated with Major Bradford, advising him that Major Booth's troops should man the interior works and he the exterior fortifications. His further instructions that "in case of attack, you will of course seek refuge in the fortification"[36] postured a clear ambiguity as it made no reference to holding the rifle pits, whose eventual abandonment Hurlbut rightfully assessed was one of the keys to the garrison's defense.

The more egregious of General Hurlbut's blunders was his failure to maintain sufficient communication with the garrison whereby the mounting of an effective relief force or additional gun boat could have been timely dispatched. Unfortunately, he did not learn until 7:00 P.M. on 12 April that the fort was under attack. Within an hour after ordering the 55th Regiment to embark upon the steamer *Glendale* with four days rations and forty rounds of ammunition per man, he received a report from another steamer that the fort had been captured. The excursion was canceled, and no further effort was undertaken to pursue Forrest.[37]

Out of frustration, General Sherman indicated to General Grant that "Forrest could pen [Hurlbut] up with 2,500 men, although Hurlbut has all of Grierson's cavalry and 2,500 white infantry, 4,000 blacks, and the citizen militia, 3,000." In ordering Hurlbut relieved, General Grant observed "Does General Hurlbut think if he moves a part of his force after the only enemy within 200 miles of him that the post will run off with the balance of his force?"[38] General Hurlbut was relieved for "marked timidity in the management of affairs since Forrest passed north of Memphis."[39] General Wasburn, with the acquiescence of Sherman, was ordered to Memphis by General Grant.

Summarizing the factors contributing to the defeat of Fort Pillow there emerges a picture of misplaced confidence, "fancied security," an "illusory element of strength," errant leadership, and inadequate strategy. The single gun boat was useless; the garrison was not experienced or strong enough to hold the advantageous positions of rifle pits and middle breast works; Major Bradford's incompetence in not attempting to thwart Confederate troop movements during the truce and his panic in the end; Major Booth's failure to appreciate the inadequate field of fire for his artillery and riflemen, and not recognizing as well the advantage the knolls provided sharpshooters; in realizing too late the hazard inherent in maintaining buildings near the main fortifications; the total command failure after the Confederates stormed over the parapets; the rampant operations of spies and Confederate sympathizers within the fort; the lack of a reliable mechanism for intelligence gathering; and the total absence of any lines of communication that would permit adequate succor to a beleaguered garrison. The defense of Fort Pillow was doomed from the beginning as a result of superior strategy, generalship, and troop deployment from outside the fortifications and reckless confidence, inferior leadership, and poor troop concentration from within.

5

An Indiscriminate Slaughter

The controversy concerning the engagement at Fort Pillow evolves upon two principle questions: Was there a deliberate slaughter of the Federal garrison? What role did General Forrest and his officers have in the affair? Historians who would acquit the Confederates and their officers of any wrongdoing have presented persuasive though not necessarily convincing arguments. Much of the rationale for their reasoning has been based upon the first-hand accounts of Confederate participants and an analysis of the voluminous records taken soon after the incident. The correspondence, reports, and testimony of the official records have been for the most part condemned by Forrest supporters as exaggerated, inconsistent, inaccurate, or the emotional accounts of propaganderists who needed a scapegoat for the Federal army's ineptitude. The report generated by the Joint Committee on the Conduct of the War's investigation, as well as the affidavits gathered by General Brayman, it is true, were hardly conducted in an atmosphere free of emotional subjectivity and outrage. Substantial political pressure from journalists and government quarters preceded the investigative team's arrival at Mound City. Though the resolution of Congress charged the Joint Committee "to inquire into the truth of the rumored slaughter," the investigative report saw their purpose as "taking testimony in regard to the massacre of Fort Pillow"; a choice of emphasis that some may view as a predisposition to the outcome.

The Congressional Report may well have been a propaganda device, the object of which was to arouse northern wrath and inflame Negro sensitivities, thereby promoting a more determined war effort. The report does contain some exaggerations and misstatements of fact and was the product of ex parte statements that avoided the scrutiny of rebuttal testimony or cross-examination. The proformer questioning admits a certain lack of probing style and searching inquisitiveness which is generally the hallmark of seasoned and tutored investigators.

Notwithstanding the hysteria that prevailed at the time and the investigative team's weaknesses, the content of the report, the testimony, documentation, and personal observations upon which it was based, are of historical value. Curiously, many who condemned the report as a distortion of the true events were not adverse to utilizing selected portions that buttressed their point of view. Moreover, testimony relied upon to express the Confederate point of view is no less riddled with inconsistencies and self-serving extrapolation. All the testimony, when viewed with a critical eye and measured against the facts accumulated after as well as known to exist before the event, contain sufficient indicia of truth to dispel the Southern charge the committee's report was a conspiracy of "suggested falsehoods,"[1] "self-contradicting" statements, "deftly woven out of the exaggerated testimony of two or three of the officers and some of the Negroes and whites who were of the garrison."[2]

Certainly, the evidence was compiled soon enough after the event as not to be considered a recent fabrication. Nor can a charge be made that the recollections were tarnished with the passage of time as may be the case with Confederate recollections. An examination of the statements reveal an apparent forthrightness to the extent that many witnesses admit to not having seen specific incidents. Any inflation of numbers of persons seen shot after the taking of the fort, where the shootings occurred, the time incidents occurred, identification of rebel officers, placing of fault, whether the black or white troops broke first, and suppositions inherent in some answers do not detract from the incontrovertible theme that a massacre occurred.

If fabrication of truth and distortion of facts were the objects of the investigation, surely the swiftness of editorial prerogative could have influenced the content of the report and the purported "prompted" answers would have had the more definite markings of a script. While there are some inconsistencies, the overall impact of the testimony is convincing and contains a general consistency woven throughout the narration that invests the whole with trustworthiness.

The investigative team chosen by the Joint Committee on the Conduct and Expenditures of the War "to investigate the late massacre at Fort Pillow" consisted of Senator Benjamin F. Wade and Representative Daniel W. Gooch. The members of the com-

mittee left Washington on 19 April and proceeded directly to
Cairo, Illinois, accompanied by a stenographer. Hearings were
held at Cairo and Mound City, Illinois; Columbus, Kentucky; Fort
Pillow and Memphis, Tennessee, during the period of 22 April
through 26 April. They interviewed or received statements from
seventy-three persons together with thirteen additional affidavits
furnished by General Brayman. Since some of the affidavits were
from persons who were also interrogated by the committee, it
would appear that of the total interviewed, fifty-one were in the
fort during the conflict, six were aboard the *New Era*, and the
remainder either came to the fort the day following the attack or
provided secondary information. As described in the report, the
scope of the committee's investigation focused on the attack, capture, and massacre at Fort Pillow and the operation of Forrest and
his command preceding and following the "horrible transaction."

The main point put forward by the committee was

> that the atrocities committed at Fort Pillow were not the result of pas-
> sions executed by the heat of conflict, but were the result of a policy
> deliberately decided upon and unhesitatingly announced. Even if the
> uncertainty of the fate of those officers and men belonging to colored
> regiments who have heretofore been taken prisoners by the rebels has
> failed to convince the authorities or our government of this fact, the tes-
> timony herewith submitted must convince even the most skeptical that it
> is the intention of the rebel authorities not to recognize the officers and
> men of our colored regiments as entitled to the treatment accorded by
> all civilized nations to prisoners of war.[3]

After summarizing the events at Union City, Paducah, and
Columbus, the committee observed that "it was at Fort Pillow,
however, that the brutality and cruelty of the rebels were most
fearfully exhibited."[4] The committee observed that misuse of the
flag of truce by Forrest's forces made the fall of the fort inevitable.
The "barbarity" and "butchery" that followed was characterized by
"an indiscriminate slaughter, sparing neither age nor sex, white or
black, soldier, or civilian" and occurred after "our men had
thrown down their arms and ceased to offer resistance." (The
entire report is quoted in appendix.) Capsuling specific incidents,
i.e., shooting hospital patients and wounded, nailing an officer to
a building that was set on fire, burning structures containing
wounded, burying some who were not dead, killing civilians, mur-
dering prisoners, continuation of the mayhem into the evening
and following morning, the committee postured, "No cruelty

which the most fiendish malignity could devise was omitted by these murderers."

Many other instances of equally atrocious cruelty might be enumerated, but your committee feel compelled to refrain from giving here more of the heartsickening details, and refer to the statements contained in the volumnious testimony herewith submitted. Those statements were obtained by them from eyewitnesses and sufferers; many of them, as they were examined by your committee, were lying upon beds of pain and suffering, some so feeble that their lips could with difficulty frame the words by which they endeavored to convey some idea of the cruelty which had been inflicted on them, and which they had seen inflicted on others.

In an article in the *Harpers New Monthly Magazine* Dr. John A. Wyeth wrote, "to one capable of reasoning without prejudice, that instead of being responsible for the great loss of life in the capture of this stronghold, Forrest did everything which a humane commander could have done to prevent it" and that "the misfortunes which befell this garrison were due in great measure to the woeful incompetency of the officers in command of the naval and military forces of the United States."[5] General Jordan, writing in 1868, opined the victims at the fort were not the result of "unlawful acts of war, . . . but of an insensate endeavor, as foolishly resolved as feebly executed, to hold a position naturally untenable and badly fortified,—the victims, we may add, in all sincerety, not of a savage ferocity on the part of their late adversaries, but of the imbecility and grievous mismanagement of those weak, incapable officers, whom the fortunes of war unhappily had placed over them."[6]

While other authors would also claim the conclusions of the congressional committee could not survive "critical examination," the principle points proffered by Forrest supporters, or Confederists, are equally patterned with imprecise analysis, bias, and lacking in historical context.

Confederists argue the accusation of a violation of the flag of truce is without basis. While previously discussed, the evidence, garnered from Forrest's official report and the statements of other members of his command together with the accounts of survivors creates undeniable proof of the truce violation. Two detachments of one hundred and fifty to possibly two hundred men each were deployed near the rear portions of the southern and northern areas of the fort perpendicular to the river when the flag was out to ostensibly prevent an approaching steamboat

from landing troops. Though these movements involved reinforcing positions partially occupied by McCulloch's forces around the
barracks and Bell's brigade along Coal Creek ravine, the deployment was hardly "superfluous."

In response to General Forrest's first demand to surrender Major Bradford asked for an hour's consultation time and "in the
meantime no preparations to be made on either side." Forrest
acknowledged in his report to President Davis that "several hours
of hard fighting" preceded the flag of truce and the desired positions were not obtained, "however, without considerable loss." The
debate is not confined to the movement of the troops under the
commands of Anderson and Barteau, but other troops moved
into the rifle pits and "crawled" into the ditch during the truce.
The consolidation of positions, "massing and disposing their
forces," and coming "up even to the ditch" at the foot of the
redoubt above which the cannons were placed were movements
unrelated to the approach of the steamboat, *Olive Branch*. Francis
Alexander, Co. C, 13th Tennessee Cavalry, swore that during the
consultation the rebels "were coming up a gap or hollow, where
we could have cut them to pieces. They tried it before, but could
not do it. I saw them come up there while the flag of truce was
in the second time."[7] Lieutenant Leaming also observed troops
moving into positions the enemy had been fighting to obtain up
until 3:30 P.M.

Colonel Barteau claimed his troops occupied the Cold Creek
Ravine prior to the truce, and any movement during the truce
was designed only to prevent the landing of Federal reinforcements. Upon the apprehension that the approaching steamer
crowded with troops would aid the fort, particularly in view of
the one hour request for consultation, rests the major argument
for justifying the Confederate troop deployment. The evidence
suggests, however, that the rebel action was in excess of the threat
and made in areas away from the potential troop landing. The
conclusion is inescapable, notwithstanding any professed concern,
the movement under the flag of truce tightened the noose, mini-
mized potential rebel casualties, made the ultimate outcome more
certain, and strengthened existing positions.

The violations of the truce, as noted earlier, were not a significant factor in the capture of the fort. The fort's capture was inevitable because of the Confederate's superior strength and Forrest's
strategy which was abetted by the errors of judgment and miscal-
culations of the Federal officers.

A second point of contention is whether an "indiscriminate

slaughter" occurred or the committee's report of a massacre merely reflected "rhetoric" to cover up the gross ineptness of the garrison and its supporting elements.[8]

Denying the report's charges and contrary to Forrest's own admission that women and children were removed with the prisoners, Henry observed all the civilians were removed by boat to an island during the early stages of the engagement. He argues had there been an order to exterminate the garrison, more casualties would have been inflicted. Moreover, since there is no accurate tally as to the wounded and killed from the initial "unerring aim of rebel sharpshooters" and "probably still heavier loss" suffered as the final assault breached the parapet, the remaining casualties were a direct result of the fort's failure to surrender.[9] The continuation of resistance after the storming of the parapets is a common Confederist theme offered to explain the heavy losses suffered by the garrison.

Jordan additionally postulates, "as always happens in places taken by storm, unquestionably some whites, as well as negroes, who had thrown down their arms, and besought quarter, were shot under the *insania belli* which invariably rages on such occasions."[10] Relying on military history, Jordan claimed there exists a custom to punish with death all those who unjustifiably defend an untenable place. These past military incidents provide precedent for putting to death even those defenders or others who throw down their arms and call for quarter. Referring to the cheapness with which human life was held in 1864, Wyeth observed "the scenes of bloodshed which stained this section of the South may well suggest the reddest days of the French Revolution."[11]

The futile resistance theory may have found examples in history, but there are no other reported happenings of wanton killing during the Civil War whose justification was measured by historical precedent. To be sure, battles were fought where the stubbornness of defenders and the intensity of the engagement made high casualties unavoidable. The storm of battle, swelling in fury as it reaches the final moments of rage, when men may be pushed beyond all sensate comprehension, does not abate with startling suddenness at the appearance of a fleeing foe. Sporadic firing may continue as the attackers come to accept the reality of victory, heed the command to disengage, or sense no further physical threat. For well-disciplined troops led by competent officers, however, the cessation of hostilities should require but a few moments after the objective is achieved; not the twenty to thirty minutes that actually occurred.

The circumstances at Fort Pillow did not demonstrate the death struggle inherent in stubborn resistance, although the failure to initially surrender may have been an obstinate jester of futility. Once the Confederates breached the defenses and the Federal command structure broke down, rather than exhibiting continued defiance, the defenders ceased their resistance and abandoned the fort, only to be pursued by troops whose objective exceeded the fort's capture.

Whatever historical incidents of comparable slaughter may be found, no precedent exists among civilized antagonists that ever gave legitimacy to the deliberate shooting of soldiers who sought to surrender. Events from other times depicting similar occurrences merely acknowledge that on the field of battle, barbarity, like history, has a repetitive quality. No stretch of logic or strained analysis can justify the events that occurred at Fort Pillow by citing similar examples of wickedness.

Wyeth claimed "The garrison had resolved to die—not to surrender. The Confederates were there to take that fort or die in the attempt. No marvel the loss of life was terrible."[12] He further asserted that the failure to lower the flag as the Federals retreated down the bluff prevented those rebels stationed below the precipice from realizing anything other than that the garrison was either trying to escape to the safety of the gunboat or to continue the fray along the river bank. The Federals, he claims, were panic stricken, without leadership, intoxicated, and in an effort to escape ran into the murderous cross fire from Anderson's and Barteau's flanking positions who were forty to one hundred yards distant,[13] while the rebels atop the bluff fired down into their midst.

Many of the survivors now realized that escape or rescue was hopeless and threw down their guns; some, wild with fright or frenzied by liquor or the wounds they had received, rushed into the river and were drowned or shot to death as they attempted to swim away. Many of the white men, more intelligent than their colored comrades, threw themselves behind logs, stumps, brush heaps, or into the gullies which they encountered in their flight, and thus saved themselves from the frightful mortality which befell the terror-stricken Negroes; some few of whom, either insanely intoxicated or convinced from the slaughter that had transpired that no quarter would be shown them, and determined to sell their lives as dearly as possible, still offered resistance and continued to fire at the Confederates. . . . Others broke through the investing lines and, refusing to halt, were pursued and killed. . . . But for the insane conduct of their drunken and desperate comrades, a great many of those who perished would have escaped.[14]

Additionally, the Confederists maintain, following the cessation of hostilities, the failure of the *New Era* to heed the truce signals of Captain Anderson who was accompanied by the fort's provost, Captain John T. Young, the seriously wounded could not be taken off until the next day. If any atrocities occurred the evening of the 12th, it had to have been the result of scoundrels and guerrillas who were frequent scavengers at the scenes of battles because the closest rebel troops were two miles from the fort.

The Confederist view that the garrison's conduct contributed to their own devastation was prompted by factors suggesting the retreat from the fort proper was a prearranged plan to continue resistance below the bluff from "prepared positions" and/or for the purpose of awaiting aid while under cover of the gun boat. In anticipation of having to abandon the breastworks, Major Bradford was supposed to have arranged a scheme with Captain Marshall of the *New Era* whereby the garrison could be succored by the gun boat until aid arrived. This theory is based upon Captain Marshall's testimony before the committee that shortly after the flag of truce was withdrawn "Major Bradford signalled to me we were whipped. We had agreed on a signal that, if they had to leave the fort, they would drop down under the bank, and I was to give the rebels canister."[15] Jordan asserted a "prearranged signal" was given, and the garrison en masse "sped down the precipitous bank" for the place of refuge.[16] Major Anderson, writing after the war, claimed a detail under his command recovered 269 Federal serviceable rifles along the bank of the river together with six open cartridge cases, which were piled against the upturned roots of an old tree.[17] This discovery is relied upon by Confederists as conclusive proof of the "insane scheme" to continue the resistance below the bluff.

The line of questioning by the committee unfortunately did not pursue Marshall's testimony concerning this prearranged plan to continue the struggle below the bluff nor were any of the survivors queried as to their knowledge regarding being aided by the gun boat. Undoubtedly, the answers were too obvious to raise the issue to the level of legitimacy. Except for Marshall's statement there is no other reference in the testimony or sworn statements giving validity to the existence of this plan. Neither is the scheme made credible by the presence of weapons below the bluff. The existence of serviceable rifles inventoried by Anderson as having been found below the bluff is as consistent with panic-stricken troops throwing away their weapons as they fled down the hill as it is suggestive of an effort to continue resistance. Even Forrest's acknowledgement of capturing 350 stand of small arms along with the six pieces of artillery is not persuasive of the Confederate perspective regarding this question. He reported "All the small-arms were picked up where the enemy fell or threw them down. A few were in the fort, the balance scattered from the top of the hill to the water's edge."[18]

An analysis of survivor accounts and the practicality of such a scheme renders the idea at best dubious, and more likely nothing other than the boastfulness of a naval officer who amplified his role beyond the limits of his actual involvement and the circumstances present.

Contrary to Jordan's unsubstantiated statement that a "prearranged signal" was given, Marshall only asserted he received a signal from Major Bradford that the garrison was "whipped." By the captain's own admission the *New Era* was out of position to render effective assistance, an accomplishment that even alluded him when his guns were active. Further, he harbored the apprehension that were he to have fired his guns he would have injured that part of the garrison who were still in the fort. It is inconceiveable that Captain Marshall, had he been in the proper position, could have rendered with the remaining seventy-five rounds of ammunition the kind of assistance he could not render with 282 previously expended shells when at least he had someone to direct where to lob the rounds. Had he been below the fort his concern for hitting "our own men" in any event would not have been different.

The plan, if it existed, would certainly have been conveyed to Major Bradford's subordinates in order to prepare for an effective withdrawal at the appropriate time. Lieutenant Leaming, who was part of Bradford's command and became post adjutant during the conflict, made no reference to this ill-conceived plan in either of his lengthy statements or testimony. In this he was not alone, for there is not even a hint in any of the testimony that the reason for leaving the fort was for the purpose of carrying out this purported scheme. In truth of fact, "necessity, not strategy, precipitated the retreat."[19]

Henry Weaver reported that "when the cavalry commenced to break our colored troops wavered, and the rebels had by this time succeeded in entering the fort. Lieutenant Van Horn begged and

Rear of Fort Pillow photographed about halfway down steep incline.

ordered them to stop, but each one sought safety in flight."[20] Others observed Major Bradford, as the rebels were scaling the works, imploring the troops "boys, save your lives." When Lieutenant Bischoff objected and pleaded with the major to order the men to remain at their posts and continue the fight, the major, "turning around and seeing the enemy coming in from all sides in overwhelming numbers, replied that it was useless."[21] Two lieutenants described the enemy "came pouring in solid masses right over the breast-works. Their numbers were perfectly overwhelming. The moment they reached the top of the walls and commenced firing the troops were panic-stricken" and throwing away their weapons "ran down the bluff, pursued sharply, begging for life, but escape was impossible."[22]

These descriptions do not betoken an orderly withdrawal for the purpose of regrouping or seeking the shelter of the bluff or the aide of the gunboat. On the contrary, it would have been impossible for these or any other troops to offer resistance once outside the fort with their backs to the water. Even one untutored in the art of warfare can appreciate that firing up a steep incline, without adequate cover, while the enemy twice your number is sending a murderous fire into your unprotected midst would be

sheer insanity. The terrain below the fort and the absence of prepared positions precluded a concentrated fire being effectively
executed by even an organized force. There was also the potential
threat that the cannons left atop the bluff could be turned on
them. Even Forrest noted the regiment that carried the fort
"poured a destructive fire into the rear of the now panic-stricken
and almost decimated garrison."[23] Forrest's observation is inconsistent with any organized resistance being carried on.

There was no plan to continue the fray below the bluff because it was not even remotely possible to execute. The withdrawal
was characteristic of a dispirited fighting force; suddenly over-
whelmed, without direction, their commanding officer bewil-
dered, they broke, fleeing instanter to escape the horde in search
of a place and a moment when the raging passions of close combat
might have abated.

Whether a plan existed to evacuate or aide the Federal forces
as they retreated below the bluff is actually of no relevance to a
Unionist's account of the battle. The Confederist theory, however,
turns on whether the troops abandoning the fort believed a plan
to afford them succor was a reality. Since the Confederates did
not know about the possibility of the purported scheme until after
publication of the Congressional Report and transcript, they
could not possibly have believed the retreat from the fort was for
the purpose of continuing resistance. In his account to President
Davis, Forrest presumed incorrectly, or misstated intentionally,
"the enemy attempted to retreat to the river, . . . either for protection of gunboats or to escape."[24] His deployment order to Anderson was limited to preventing the *Olive Branch* from landing
reinforcements and to not allowing the Federals to escape along
the river bank. He well knew there was only one gun boat on the
scene during the final assault which was offering no assistance
and was too far off shore to safely remove the garrison alone or
towing the two barges cabled to the shore. The possibility of escape was rendered moot by the troops he stationed along the
river bank. The significance then of Forrest's statement "the
slaughter was heavy" is that those who would proffer a theory
no massacre occurred could find justification for the inordinate
shooting that took place on the reverse slope of the bluff and at
the water's edge, although the *New Era* posed no threat during
those desperate moments and further resistance was at best im-
practical.

The retreat from the fort occurred with such alacrity that the
Union flag continued to fly from its mast. The garrison's failure

to lower the flag does not give further proof of an ill-advised defiance to continue the fight or a refusal to surrender, thereby providing additional justification for the heavy casualties. Quite simply, in their haste to flee, neither officers nor enlisted men had the presence of mind to strike the colors. This inadvertence is hardly implausible, since in the excitement of the morning's initial attack an entire hour elapsed before Lieutenant Leaming noticed the Federal flag had not been raised.[25]

No sooner had Forrest seen his men gain the parapet and jump in among the defenders then he immediately galloped from his position atop a knoll some four hundred yards outside of the fort. The order for all firing to cease was announced after a private from Barteau's regiment had cut the halyards and the fallen flag was handed to the general.[26] According to Forrest the lowering of the flag was a fortunate occurrence for the survivors as "[t]he force stationed in the rear of the fort could see the flag, but were too far under the bluff to see the fort, and when the flag descended they ceased firing; but for this, so near were they to the enemy, that few, if any, would have survived unhurt another volley."[27] Except Gus, if ordered by General Forrest, could have sounded a spirited recall on his bugle at any time. The flag was not the focal point of the attack. When the garrison came storming out of the fort, the battle was over. Those rebels stationed to the rear of the fort, either near Cold Creek or the steamboat landing, did not have to observe the lowering of the Union flag to know the garrison was finished as an effective fighting force. The Confederates atop of the bluff certainly knew the battle was over when they reached the edge of the hill and the fort's capture was complete. The scene of scattering, disorganized troops, abandoning their positions, stumbling down the hill and jumping into the river, throwing away their guns, pleading for mercy, and otherwise offering no resistance was enough to signal the end of the conflict. The Confederates continued to fire into the hapless Federal troops because in the main no quarter was to be given and the cessation of shooting was not to be ordered until the commanding general and his men satiated their need to render retribution and teach the garrison of fugitive slaves and traitorous Tennesseeans a few lessons.

Proponents of the theory no massacre occurred, or at worst, it was unintentional, claim the disportionate number of casualties between the contending forces can be understood when one considers the drunken condition of the garrison. According to Henry "there is abundant testimony from Confederate sources that widespread and almost general intoxication among the garrison contributed to the frenzy of the scattered resistance offered between the time the parapet was stormed and the time Forrest could restore order below the bluffs."[28] Relying solely upon "the sworn testimony of honorable and trustworthy men," the disputed fact is established "beyond contradiction" that the condition of intoxication prevailed among a large portion of the garrison.[29]

The affidavits obtained by Dr. Wyeth from five Confederate officers and attested to by fifty other Confederates who participated in the battle were accumulated thirty-four years after the event. None of the facts described in the affidavits ever found reference in any of the official reports these same officers submitted contemporaneous with the battle.

Among the statements, General Chalmers swore "those of the garrison who were sober enough to realize the hopelessness of their situation after the fort was stormed, surrendered, and thus escaped being killed or wounded." Brigadier Tyree H. Bell, under oath, claimed "Our troops never fired a gun until they landed inside the fort. The firing lasted not exceeding three minutes, and there was no more firing from either side. I went over the parapet with my men, and the first thing I noticed after the firing ceased was three or four vessels of whiskey with tin cups attached" which was immediately ordered overturned. Colonel Robert McCulloch, commanding the left wing of the Confederate assault, also attested to the presence of alcohol. "The presence of open whiskey barrels within the fort, together with the conduct of the troops after the Confederates carried the works, showed plainly that a large proportion of the garrison were under the influence of liquor at the time of the assault." Colonel C. R. Barteau, who commanded the Second Tennessee of Bell's brigade near the Cold Creek Ravine, observed "They were in a frenzy of excitement or drunken delirium. Some even, who had thrown down their arms, took them up again and continued firing." Major Charles W. Anderson attributed the garrison's heavy losses during the retreat to three factors: "the incapacity of their commander, the drunken condition of the men, and the fatal agreement with and promise of Captain Marshall of the New Era to protect and succor them when driven from the works."[30]

Summarizing this testimony Dr. Wyeth observed, "To those familiar with the two classes, black and white, which composed the bulk of the private soldiers in the garrison at Fort Pillow, and their fondness for intoxicating drinks, especially so with the Negroes just free from slavery, it will readily be accepted, that they did not fail to take advantage of the opportunities here offered to drink to excess. Their conduct during the truce and the insane resistance beneath the bluff bear out the allegations that many were intoxicated."[31]

This ad hominen appeal to racial prejudice and a remonstrance that has its basis in the purported impeccable authority of self-serving declarants is hardly anchored in logic and fact. The sworn statements of these officers are impeachable and either intentionally false, or they contain recollections whose accuracy is rendered suspect by the passage of thirty-four years. General Bell, who is one of only two persons who claim to have actually seen the "vessels of whiskey," swore that after storming the parapet the firing from both sides lasted just three minutes. This time frame is at substantial variance with all other Confederate participant recollections that fix the duration of fighting from twenty to thirty minutes.

The drunken garrison theory is merely a fabrication of distorted facts. Dr. C. Fitch, a surgeon at the fort, wrote a letter in 1879 defending General Chalmers. General Chalmers, then a congressman, was being assailed on the floor of the Congress for his participation in the "Fort Pillow Massacre." Praising Chalmers for protecting him, Dr. Fitch stated that after being taken up the bluff and passing outside the earthworks he met a few ambulances with their drunken, cowardly crew. They were about to take off the doctor's boots when General Chalmers interceded.

> I am not aware that there was any formal surrender of Fort Pillow to Forrest's command. I looked upon many things that were done as the result of whiskey and a bitter personal hate, especially as regards the Thirteenth regiment. There was considerable alcohol outside the fort, which Forrest's men must have got hold of long before the charge was made. I have always thought that neither you nor Forrest knew anything that was going on at the time under the bluffs. What was done was done very quickly.[32]

Even Dr. Wyeth acknowledged some of the Confederates had obtained whiskey. "About an hour before the assault was made a detachment of Forrest's command posted at the extreme left of his line broke into the quartermaster's stores, which had been captured at this time, and before they could be compelled to quit the building had had access to a supply of whiskey which they discovered there. The moment Forrest learned that his men were pillaging the captured stores he rode there rapidly and put a stop to it personally."[33] The testimony of several witnesses confirms that McCulloch's men on the "extreme left" had access to this liquor supply.[34] Several Federal participants observed the pillaging of the quartermaster's department. At the time the Confederates had access to these buildings, there was nothing to prevent them from also raiding the hotel, sutler cabins, or sundry stores located in the town where casks of beer, cheese, and crackers could be found. Concededly, there is no proof in the record this latter looting occurred before the final assault.

Neither army's official reports of the engagement or the observations of military, civilian, and newspaper reporters arriving on the scene the following day contained any reference to the insobriety of the garrison or described physical evidence the garrison consumed alcohol in order to animate their courage in the face of the enemy's perilous advance.

During the period of 1976–78, extensive archaeological excavations were conducted in and around the fort and its environs. Some remains of wine and beer bottles were recovered as were evidence of the presence of Dr. J. Hostetter's Celebrated Stomach Bitters. Dr. Hostetter's popular tonic contained alcohol and was distributed to the Union Army early in the war. Three fragmentary examples of possibly twenty-eight-ounce bottles were found.[35] These shards of proof are hardly determinative of the question, and any conclusions drawn from the recovered items would be mere speculation. Most assuredly, had there been clear proof of even some of the garrison's consumption of alcohol, General Chalmers and others, while aboard the *Platte Valley* or touring the fort with observers, would have brought this to the attention of their Federal hosts when queried as to the fate of the troops. Why would Chalmers have claimed he could not control his men as long as the Federals insisted upon making soldiers out of slaves when he enthusiastically could have given indisputable proof of the freeman's penchant for liquor? The drunken garrison theory is just another disingenuous attempt to deflect the truth and avoid any disparagement of Forrest or his troops. That Federal troops would make use of alcohol or their officers approve such consumption during a battle can only be accorded the accolade of pure fantasy. If buckets with ladles were present, they were filled with water. Just as Confederates were seen obtaining water from Cold Creek, Union troops had a similar thirst and need during battle.

An examination of the development of black troops and their officers in the U.S. Army renders the drunken garrison theory ludicrous. While exceptions can be found, the overall calibre of officers and soldiers serving in black units were equal to their peers on either side of the conflict in terms of their military discipline.

When the war broke out, blacks from both the North and South knew the conflict provided an opportunity to prove their worth as men and break the chains of 243 years of bondage. The idea of blacks under arms was anathema to many northerners and peculiarly repugnant to southerners. Racism of course was not confined by territorial boundaries in 1861 but found expression throughout the country. The prevalent differences in attitude were defined more in the extent of tolerance and the expressions of hatred as practiced in the different regions of the country. Compelling practical considerations, however, finally silenced the debate in the north over arming blacks.

Brigadier General Benjamin Butler is credited as one of the first Union commanders to employ blacks in the army. He accepted three runaway slaves at Fortress Monroe as contraband, no different than other spoils of war, and put them to work in the Union Army building a bakery. In this manner he shrewdly created an exception to the Fugitive Slave Law, which required runaway slaves be returned to their masters, and established precedent for incorporating blacks into military service.[36] Other individual efforts from within and outside the military would give impetus to the arming of blacks.

Subsequent to the Emancipation Proclamation, the War Department in May 1863 created the Bureau of Colored Troops for the purpose of raising black troops and securing officers. While the Proclamation only applied to states considered "in rebellion against the United States," its impact was felt in states like Tennessee, which was not considered as belligerent in 1863. The Bureau of Colored Troops was an ambitious experiment that, though not among the stated purposes, had the effect of using the armed services as a vehicle for eventually reforming racial stereotypes.[37]

Officer positions were reserved for whites and candidates were required to pass a fairly rigorous review designed to weed out those who did not possess the dedication, seriousness of purpose, and military experience and knowledge required. There were nine thousand applicants for commands, and of the four thousand who took the examination only 60 percent were granted commissions.[38] Although motives varied and not always altruistic reasons promoted interest in these commands,[39] the overall impact of this selective process was to create an officer core which for the most part had been in combat—seen the "elephant"—and could accept the fatal consequences under Confederate law for leading blacks under arms. It is against this background that one is to accept that the officers of black units would jeopardize their lives as well as their commands by distributing liquor prior to combat.

Although the enlisted men who filled the ranks of black units assigned to Fort Pillow were for the most part illiterate and the product of slave environments they enlisted for less than eleemosynary reasons. They, too, were aware the usual principles of war applicable to prisoners did not apply to them and at best, if captured they could only hope to be returned to slavery or pressed into the hard labor of building fortifications. "It required more courage of Negroes than for Whites to become soldiers, because the Confederacy had not revoked its stated intention to punish captured Negroes as insurrectionists."[40] Their enlistment was more personal than love of country, it was to destroy that pernicious institution—slavery. The participation of the black soldier was "a holy struggle for human liberty"[41] that could not be compromised or needed to be inflamed by the consumption of alcohol. If "the wildest confusion prevailed"[42] among those below the bluff or the garrison "acted like a crowd of drunken men,"[43] it was the general effect that receiving no quarter had upon them; the intoxicant hate, not alcohol, was the cause for the disorder. Hardy Revelle, a civilian who participated in the defense, stated "when we found there was no quarter to be shown, and that (white and black) we were to be butchered, we also gave up our arms and passed down the hill."[44] Stamps claimed the soldiers retreating from the fort were "saying the rebels were showing no quarter." John Penwell, another civilian, who was inside the fort when the rebels poured in, claimed after firing his last shot, he saw the rebels running "right up to us." He threw down his musket, and "a fellow who was ahead asked 'if I surrender,' I said, 'Yes.' He said, 'Die, then, you damned Yankee son of a bitch, and shot me, and I fell."[45] From the *New Era* Dr. Chapman Underwood, assistant surgeon at the fort, saw no resistance after the fort was seized, but many were shot below the bluff who had surrendered.[46] Acting Master Ferguson, who arrived at Fort Pillow on the *Silver Cloud* the day after the attack, claimed all the wounded he spoke to agreed that following the fort's capture an "indiscriminate slaughter" took place and "on every side horrible testimony to the truth of this statement could be seen."[47] If any firing by Federals occurred below the bluff, it could only have been inspired by the unrelenting fire of the rebels who were not giving quarter, rather than by a design to continue the resistance. If "wild confusion" prevailed, the reason is self-evident.

During the time the flag of truce was out, the troops were so close "that the white men of both sides were bantering each other from their respective positions, while some of the negroes indulged in provoking, impudent jeers."[48] McCulloch's men who had come out from behind the barracks and houses at this time were met with challenges from blacks who had mounted the parapet for them to try and take the fort. Epithets were hurled at the Confederates "couched in most obscene and abusive terms and accompanied by gestures and actions not to be described."[49] Undoubtedly, the taunting and derisive remarks hurled from the fort only exacerbated the resentment of seeing former slaves facing their masters with arms in hand. The scene could only have inflamed the passions involved in the killing frenzy that was to follow.

Notwithstanding the arguments presented by those who claimed either no massacre occurred or the large number of casualties were a result of the garrison's conduct, the sifted testimony of witnesses describes a common theme of uncommon mayhem. Of twenty-one blacks, twelve of whom acknowledged being former slaves, eighteen claimed to have been shot after they surrendered. Eighteen survivors from the 13th Tennessee Cavalry were interviewed by the committee, and twelve insisted they were shot after they surrendered. In both categories several were also shot before the surrender. While there was never a formal surrender, numerous efforts by individuals and sufficient tokens of surrender demonstrated that after fleeing the fort proper the garrison had given up any further resistance. Approximately thirty-five witnesses saw shootings after the surrender. Practically all the wounded received some injury below the bluff or when climbing back up the hill. Although the Congressional Report testimony revealed not all the Confederate officers were involved,[50] many of those interviewed saw officers participating in the massacre or heard officers giving the orders.[51]

Several of the witnesses stated that the shooting of wounded prisoners was not limited to the day of the battle, but continued into the evening and the following day.[52] Nor were the victims limited to combatants. Several reports claimed women and children were either wounded or killed.[53] There is no accurate means for ascertaining civilian casualties and even Forrest's estimates are exaggerated. The facts reveal not all the civilians were removed in the morning by the *Liberty*. Witness statements and the burning of the contraband camp indicate substantial numbers of wounded and killed occurred among the civilians. One wounded female was treated at Mound City, and one white female was found buried among the dead.[54] One young black boy was shot, possibly, on the orders of General Chalmers.[55] On the day after the battle, Lieutenant Clary saw a Confederate officer shoot a man coming down a hill, which may have been the same incident described by Captain Ferguson of the *Silver Cloud.*

Dr. Fitch, who is remembered for having tendered an affidavit on behalf of General Chalmers, related to Lieutenant Clary that the Confederates did not respect his hospital flags set up below the bluff.[56] There is strong evidence and eyewitness accounts that numerous killings occurred in the hospital building itself where not only some of the early wounded had gone but where convalesants were recovering.[57] The testimony revealed that a building holding several black soldiers was allegedly bolted from the outside and set afire. Admittedly tents were burned the following day. The only dispute is whether the men inside had died as a result of their wounds or because the tents were torched.[58] Charred remains of some of the garrison were found in the ruins with a few having been nailed through their clothing to the floors of the torched structures.[59]

Two men were buried alive.[60] One Confederate soldier wrote in the Atlanta Appeal on 14 June 1864 about the veracity of this accusation.

You have heard that our soldiers buried Negroes alive at Fort Pillow. This is true. At the first fire, after Forrest's men scaled the walls, many of the Negroes threw down their arms and fell as if they were dead. They perished in the pretence, and could only be restored at the point of the bayonet. To resuscitate some of them, more terrified than the rest, they were rolled into the trenches made as receptacles for the fallen. Vitality was not restored until breathing was obstructed, and then the resurrection began. On these facts is based the pretext for the crimes committed by Sturgis, Grierson and their followers. You must remember too, that in the extremity of their terror, or for other reasons, the Yankess and Negroes in Fort Pillow neglected to haul down their flag. In truth, relying upon their gunboats, the officers expected to annihilate our forces after we had entered the fortifications. They did not intend to surrender.

A terrible retribution, in any event, has befallen the ignorant, deluded Negroes.[61]

The chief surgeon in charge of the Mound City Hospital, Dr.

Horace Wardner, observed that the wounded under his care were among the "worst butchered men I have ever seen." He particularly noted a sixteen-year-old black youth who had his head "hacked" open by a sabre while he lay infirm in the fort's hospital. In assessing the injuries of the wounded in the wards he noted, "there were more body wounds than in ordinary battle" and concluded the men had been shot deliberately with the intention of hitting the body.[62] Testifying on 25 April at Fort Pillow, one of the survivors, Sergeant Henry F. Weaver, a white noncommissioned officer from Co. C, 6th U.S. Heavy Artillery, recalled "I saw yesterday afternoon a great number of cavalry taken up, and almost every one was shot in the head. A great many of them looked as if their heads had been beaten in."[63]

Captain John G. Woodruff, who arrived at the fort aboard the *Platte Valley*, recounted his observations to General Brayman. He saw the bodies of fifteen blacks who had been shot through the head and the bodies of two burning. "Some of them were burned as if by powder around the holes in their heads, which led me to conclude that they were shot at very close range."[64] Acting Master Ferguson, in emotionally graphic style, recounted his experience.

Bodies with gaping wounds, some bayoneted through the eyes, some with skulls beaten through, others with hideous wounds, as if their bowels had been ripped open with Bowie knives, plainly told that but little quarter was shown to our troops, strewn from the fort to the river bank, in the ravines and hollows, behind logs and under the brush, where they had crept for protection from the assassins who pursued them . . . showing how cold-blooded and persistent was the slaughter of our unfortunate troops.[65]

If these summaries are not convincing as to the extent of the terrible slaughter practiced upon the Federal garrison at Fort Pillow, perhaps the firsthand accounts of Confederate participants will settle the point. Sergeant Achilles V. Clark of the 20th Tennessee Cavalry took part in the battle. His description of the events can hardly be considered the contrived utterances of a disgruntled rebel for he continued his military career with Forrest's forces until the end of the war and received promotion to the rank of captain. In writing to his sisters two days after the engagement, he described the scene his brigade witnessed after storming the fortification from the right.

At 2 P.M. Gen. Forrest demanded a surrender and gave twenty minutes to consider. The Yankees refused theatening that if we charged their breast works to show no quarter. The bugle sounded the charge and in less than ten minutes we were in the fort hurling the cowardly villians howling down the bluff. Our men were so exasperated by the Yankees' threats of no quarter that they gave but little. The Slaughter was awful. Words cannot describe the scene. The poor deluded negros would run up to our men fall upon their knees and with uplifted hands scream for mercy but they were ordered to their feet and then shot down. The white men fared but little better. Their fort turned out to be a great slaughter pen—blood—human blood stood about in pools and brains could have been gathered up in any quantity. I with several others tried to stop the butchery and at one time had partially succeeded, but Gen. Forrest ordered them shot down like dogs—and the carnage continued—Finally our men became sick of blood and the firing ceased.[66]

Another rebel described the battle's aftermath as "decidedly the most horrible sight that I have ever witnessed."[67]

James Walls, a private in Company E, 13th Tennessee Cavalry, informed the Congressional Committee of his personal observations.

I saw them make lots of niggers stand up, and then they shot them down as hogs. The next morning I was lying around there waiting for the boat to come up. The secesh would be prying around there, and would come to a nigger and say, "You ain't dead, are you?" They would not say anything, and then the secesh would get down off their horses, prick them in their sides, and say, "Damn you, you ain't dead, get up." Then they would make them get up on their knees, when they would shoot them down like hogs.[68]

In examining the statements of witnesses from both sides, one is struck by the similarity in intensity of description. To a reader unrestricted by regional pride or prejudiced by predisposition, these statements would suggest the evidence upon which the Congressional Committee drew its conclusion was not without basis in fact and transcended, as well, military affiliation.

According to several historians, proof positive no massacre occurred was to be found in the absence of any retaliatory policy pronounced by Federal authorities. The retaliation theory hinges on General Sherman's failure to recommend any retribution.

Four days following the fall of Fort Pillow, Secretary of War Stanton requested Sherman "direct a competent officer to investigate and report minutely, and as early as possible, the facts in relation to the alleged butchery of our troops at Fort Pillow."[69] General Sherman directed General Brayman to designate a good officer to examine witnesses and make a "full report of all the circumstances attending the capture of Fort Pillow, more especially as to the perpetration of unusual cruelties to prisoners of war, whether white or black."[70] On the day preceding this correspondence Sherman wrote Grant that he could "pen Forrest up, but it will take some time to run him down" and did Grant desire him to "delay" the campaign for that purpose.[71] In the evening of 15 April, General Grant emphatically replied "Your preparation for the coming campaign must go on, but if it is necessary [to drive Forrest out] to detach a portion of the troops intended for it, detach them and make your campaign with that much fewer men." The same correspondence contained the admonition concerning Fort Pillow that "If our men have been murdered after capture, retaliation must be resorted to promptly."[72]

Confederists maintain, since Sherman was furnished with a copy of General Brayman's investigation and was undoubtedly aware of the Congressional Committee's report, the omission to order retaliation was a clear indication Sherman did not believe the truth or acknowledge the substance of the allegations. Contemporary writers like Shelby Foote conclude that had he believed otherwise, "with Sherman in charge, retaliation would have been as prompt as even Grant could have desired."[73] Sherman, according to Ralph Selph Henry, "was not a man to shrink from ordering retaliations had he felt that it was justified."[74] Indeed, of all the Federal generals, Sherman would be the last to "shrink" from proclaiming retaliation. In fact, General Sherman, a ruthless commander in his own right, was not opposed to employing means deviating from the usual rules of engagement.

Responding to the threat of sabotage aboard riverboats, for example, General Sherman suggested he would not hesitate to authorize steamboat captains to drop overboard "mischievous characters" among their crew and "let them find the bottom in their own way," or authorize shooting on the spot any crew man caught attempting to fire a boat or placing on board powder charged fuel. He accepted the philosophy that "self-preservation, being a law of nature, will justify any means of prevention, and our prisons and courts should not be embarrassed by men who would resort to such means of carrying on war."[75] On still other occasions, Sherman was not opposed to employing unconventional means to deal with what he perceived as the aberrant war conduct of his adversaries. On the road to Savannah he deployed prisoners along the line of march to dig out "torpedoes," which had seriously injured one of his officers.[76] These antipersonnel devices were actually eight-inch shells planted in the road with friction-matches to explode when trodden on by horses. In order to deter civilians from aiding guerrilla bands, Sherman did not hesitate to encourage a subordinate to "kill a few [secessionists] at random."[77]

While General Sherman may have had doubts about Forrest's participation in the incident, based on Forrest's reputation of caring for prisoners, most definitely General Sherman did not discount the several reports and accounts he read concerning the affair. He was confident Forrest's men "acted like a set of barbarians, shooting down the helpless negro garrison after the fort was in their possession." He was "told" Forrest disclaimed any active participation in the affair, and stopped the firing as soon as practical. Although he assumed correctly that Forrest did not lead the assault but was "to the rear and out of sight if not of hearing at the time," Sherman did not seem to realize Forrest was inside the fort within minutes after the final assault commenced. There was an awareness, nevertheless, that Forrest "had a desperate set of fellows under him, and at that very time there is no doubt the feeling of the Southern people was fearfully savage on this very point of our making soldiers out of their late slaves, and Forrest may have shared the feeling."[78] Retaliation, however, posed as much of a dilemma as it promised to satiate the need for retribution or a desire to establish a deterrent policy.

The reluctance to formalize a retaliation policy was consistent with General Order No. 100, which was published on 24 April 1863 as instructions for Federal armies in the field.[79] These orders provided the first formalized document describing articles of conduct for the prosecution of war. Paragraphs twenty-seven through twenty-nine disclose why a pronouncement of retaliation was more easily demanded than effectively implemented.

27. The law of war can no more wholly dispense with retaliation than can the law of nations, of which it is a branch. Yet civilized nations acknowledge retaliation as the sternest feature of war. A reckless enemy often leaves to his opponent no other means of securing himself against the repetition of barbarous outrage.

28. Retaliation will therefore never be resorted to as a measure of mere revenge, but only as a means of protective retribution, and moreover cautiously and unavoidably—that is to say, retaliation shall only be resorted to after careful inquiry into the real occurrence and the character of the misdeeds that may demand retribution. Unjust or inconsiderate retaliation removes the belligerents farther and farther

from the mitigating rules of regular war, and by rapid steps leads them nearer to the internecine wars of savages.

29. Modern times are distinguished from earlier ages by the existence at one and the same time of many nations and great governments related to one another in close intercourse.

Peace is their normal condition; war is the exception. The ultimate object of all modern war is a renewed state of peace. The more vigorously wars are pursued the better it is for humanity. Sharp wars are brief.[80]

General Sherman had attempted what he could to avenge the stain of misdeeds practiced at Fort Pillow. He had ordered General Sturgis to pursue Forrest and "whip" him and for General McPherson to descend a force from Cairo to "strike at Forrest inland."[81] Although these plans did not have the immediate success desired, a stated policy of retaliation could not be announced without provoking the evils enumerated in General Order No. 100 and perhaps, weakening preparation for his pending historic march. General Sherman well knew reprisals were not an easily controlled strategy in war. The mayhem of war could have been elevated to new heights of ruthlessness were reprisals the order of the day. It was hardly politic to proffer a policy of reprisals, whose sword was two-edged and could have penetrated all theaters of operation. Retaliation "worked in limited circumstances only" and was, "with some exceptions, a complete failure"[82] during the Civil War. The only effective way to avoid offensive excesses was "by a successful prosecution of the war."[83]

General Sherman fully understood Lincoln's predicament when referring to Fort Pillow the president postured, "It will be a matter of grave consideration in what exact course to apply to retribution; but in the supposed case, it must come."[84] Five days after Lincoln's speech, General Sherman gave a clear indication of a policy that the government could tacitly approve. Writing to Secretary Stanton about the progress of the Fort Pillow investigation, he said:

I know well the animus of the Southern soldiery, and the truth is they cannot be restrained. The effect will be of course to make the negroes desperate, and when in turn they commit horrid acts of retaliation we will be relieved of the responsibility. Thus far negroes have been comparatively well behaved, and have not committed the horrid excesses and barbarities which the Southern papers so much dreaded. . . .

I doubt the wisdom of any fixed rule by our Government, but let soldiers affected make their rules as we progress. We will use their own logic against them, as we have from the beginning of the war.

The Southern army, which is the Southern people, cares no more for our clamor than the idle wind, but they will heed the slaughter that will follow as the natural consquence of their own inhuman acts.[85]

The conclusion is inescapable, General Sherman's refusal to elaborate a policy of retaliation was deliberate and with a conscious awareness of how reprisals would occur. No stated policy of reprisal could gain the retribution desired and only additional retaliation would follow, but incidents would occur, whose inspiration would be found in the festering, private anthem of individual soldiers—"Remember Fort Pillow."

A thorough examination of the congressional record reveals no significant contradiction or contrivance in the testimony, and the atrocities appear undeniably real. The proof is clear and convincing that on 12 April 1864, a massacre of the Federal garrison at Fort Pillow occurred soon after the Confederates stormed over the parapets. Initially, the rebels proceeded with such ferocity that "Gabriel's trumpet" was not to be heard for "thirty minutes"[86] and continued sporadically into the early evening and following morning. This result was the conscious objective of the participants, encouraged and given direction by persons in the highest positions of authority in the command structure.

That incidents similar to Fort Pillow did and would occur throughout the war was not the product of unrelated events or chance occurrences. The sociological impact upon Southern white society of over two hundred years of nurturing the institution of slavery cultivated attitudes covering the whole panoply of odious racial stereotypes and mindless bigotry. As a predominately agrarian culture, the economic implications for maintaining slavery were enormous for the South, particularly among that minority of powerfully wealthy people dependent upon slavery for retaining their political influence and social status. Other, less financially secure segments of southern society also harbored a deep disdain for the black race and echoed the same anxiety should blacks become freemen.

"The great and abiding fear of the South was of slave revolt." The South was obsessed with the possibility of slave insurrection and "any suggestion of arming the slaves by the North was as extreme as that obsession was profound."[87] A slave under arms was the realization of the South's worst nightmare; a paranoia that envisioned every conceivable degradation as a consequence. When the North began enlisting blacks into the Federal service, the South perceived this as a conspiracy to set the slaves against their masters. As early as 30 November 1862 the Confederate government was called upon to resolve the problem of slaves taken in Federal uniform. Every slave-holding state made slave insurrection punishable by death. James A. Seddon, Confederate secretary of war, in consultation with Jefferson Davis, emphatically described to General Beauregard the government's uncompromising position. Slaves in rebellion

> cannot be recognized in any way as soldiers subject to the rules of war and to trial by military courts; yet for example and to repress any spirit of insubordination it is deemed essential that slaves in armed insurrection should meet condign punishment. Summary execution must therefore be inflicted on those taken . . . under circumstances indicative beyond doubt of actual rebellion. To guard, however, against the possible abuse of this grave power under the immediate excitement of capture or through over-zeal on the part of subordinate officers it is deemed judicious that the discretion of deciding and giving the order of execution should be reposed in the general commanding the special locality of the capture.[88]

The Emancipation Proclamation was the most provocative and convincing demonstration of this northern conspiracy. Addressing the Senate and House of Representatives of the Confederate States on 12 January 1863, President Davis expressed his outrage over Lincoln's 1 January edict.

> We may well leave it to the instincts of that common humanity which a beneficent Creator has implanted in the breasts of our fellowmen of all countries to pass judgment on a measure by which several millions of human beings of an inferior race, peaceful and contented laborers in their sphere, are doomed to extermination, while at the same time they are encouraged to a general assassination of their masters by the insidious recommendation "to abstain from violence unless in necessary self-defense." Our own detestation of those who have attempted the most execrable measure recorded in the history of guilty man is tempered by profound contempt for the impotent rage which it discloses. So far as regards the action of this Government on such criminals as may attempt its execution, I confine myself to informing you that I shall, unless in your wisdom you deem some other course more expedient, deliver to the several State authorities all commissioned officers of the United States that may hereafter be captured by our forces in any of the States embraced in the proclama-

tion that they may be dealt with in accordance with the laws of those States providing for the punishment of criminals engaged in exciting servile insurrection. The enlisted soldiers I shall continue to treat as unwilling instruments in the commission of these crimes and shall direct their discharge and return to their homes on the proper and usual parole.[89]

Taking up the cudgels of an outraged public, the Confederate Congress issued a joint resolution dated 1 May 1863 pertaining to the "subject of retaliation." Since the Federal policy regarding emancipation of slaves would "if successful produce atrocious consequences" and "bring on a servile war," such active measures as are undertaken by the Federal government "may therefore be properly and lawfully repressed by retaliation." Paragraph four of the resolution provided

> That every white person being a commissioned officer or acting as such who during the present war shall command negroes or mulattoes in arms against the Confederate States or who shall arm, train, organize, or prepare negroes or mulattoes for military service against the Confederate States or who shall voluntarily aid negroes or mulattoes in any military enterprise, attack or conflict in such service shall be deemed as inciting servile insurrection, and shall if captured be put to death or be otherwise purnished at the discretion of the court.[90]

Blacks apprehended while engaged in war or giving aid to the Federals, were to be delivered to the authorities of the state where captured and dealt with according to the laws of that state.

These actions of "retaliation" by the Confederate government found precedent in Confederate War Department Order Number 60, published 21 August 1862. This document denominated specific Federal officers as "outlaws" and any commissioned officer engaged in preparing slaves for armed service was not to be regarded as a prisoner of war, but held in confinement for possible execution as a felon.[91] By April 1864 the Confederacy had not retreated from its position that Federal officers commanding African Americans were outlaws or that captured slaves were property.[92]

The attitude projected by the Confederate government reflected the regional hysteria and bitterness toward arming blacks which was endemic throughout the southern states. The "animus of the Southern soldiery" was not restricted to the infantryman, but was expressed by the Confederate officer corps as well. In the case of General Forrest, the war was not being fought for Southern independence but for the maintainence of a natural social order whose extinction would have dire monetary consequences for him. When it was suggested that the war had political implications, he responded, "If we aint fightin' fer slavery then I'd like to know what we are fightin' fer"; an attitude consistent with his understanding not to treat slaves under arms as soldiers.[93] Surely, Forrest was aware of the public position of his government regarding armed blacks and their white officers, and he harbored no less a resentment than his contemporaries for the unlawful confiscation of property and the temerous arming of blacks against their masters. As commanding general at Fort Pillow, it was within his judicious discretion to apply "condign punishment" through summary execution.

But the wrath of General Forrest and his men was not directed only to former slaves under arms. There were the renegade Tennesseans whose indecencies practiced on local civilians demanded redress. Those Tennesseans who sided with the Federals were stigmatized as "home-made Yankees," and "Torries," and "Tennessee Unionists." They were despised for not only opposing the Confederacy but destituting the countryside and causing physical harm to Confederate sympathizers. Many of the men who comprised the 13th Tennessee Cavalry were known deserters from the Confederate army and Forrest's very own command.

Lieutenant General S. D. Lee acknowledged that among the several "aggravated circumstances" bringing about the garrison's losses was "a servile race, armed against their masters and in a country which had been desolated by almost unprecedented outrages."[94]

As General Chalmers later boasted, Fort Pillow presented an opportunity to teach "the mongrel garrison of blacks and renegades a lesson long to be remembered," an objective no less indulged in by General Forrest.[95] Indeed, among the stated purposes for the incursion into Western and Northern Tennessee was Forrest's desire to apprehend deserters.

Lieutenant Rawley, remembered as "Mollie," informed Major Booth that if Forrest got possession the Federal forces and particularly the officers would be badly treated. The basis for this prediction was the statement by the individual who was granted permission by Major Booth to leave the fort, and who advised Rawley that Forrest was coming "to take the place" and "he would teach them a lesson."

In explaining the inordinate number of men killed or wounded at Fort Pillow, Ralph Henry suggests feelings between the combatants were "intensified by the bitter animosities, many of them personal, existing between the Tennessee white Unionist defenders of the fort and the assailants, and by the feeling of many Confederate soldiers toward those whom they looked upon as slaves in blue uniforms."[96] Wyeth, who conceded some Federals were shot down while trying to surrender, wrote, "this was the first occasion on which the Negro troops came prominently to notice in conflict with their late masters."[97]

Other contemporary historians also argue that Forrest's troops at Fort Pillow "had never before faced blacks in combat."[98] Most of the Confederate troops engaged in the assault, it is true, had not previously fought blacks. The defeat at Paducah, however, in which blacks played a major role in the stubborn and effective resistance of the Federals and in which Forrest was present with his escort, must have been known to the officers and men who comprised the attacking forces at Fort Pillow.

Besides the rage over the Union policy of arming blacks, the case for avenging abuses suffered by the local inhabitants cannot be understated.

Some of Bradford's men were known deserters from the Confederate Army. Others were men from the country who harbored deep resentment toward Confederate soldiers and their families. While searching the countryside for arms and rebel soldiers, Bradford and detachments of his men were accused of robbing the people of their horses, mules, beef cattle, housewares, clothing, money, and other articles of value. Further, they were accused of "venting upon the wives and daughters of Southern soldiers the most opprobrious and obscene epithets, with more than one extreme outrage upon the persons of these victims of their hate and lust."

The families of many of Forrest's men having been grievously wronged, and in some cases physically abused, some of Forrest's officers together with the citizens of Jackson and the surrounding area petitioned to form a brigade to be left behind to protect the inhabitants from further molestation. Forrest could not afford to detach a brigade, but he was "determined to employ his present resources for the summary suppressions of the evil and grievances complained of, by the surprise, if possible, and capture, at all hazards, of Fort Pillow."[99]

Atrocious incidents were reported to Forrest when he arrived at Jackson in March. Despoliation he had observed on route.[100] Forrest reported that the people have been "stripped of everything" and have "neither blacks or stock with which to raise a crop or make a support." Between the suffering of the loyal Tennesseans, looting and burning of their property, the arrests and murders, there was much perceived justification by Forrest and his forces to seek revenge.

When Forrest wrote on 4 April that he would "attend to" Fort Pillow in a few days, he knew exactly the full extent of his scheme. Fort Pillow was a military adventure he well suspected, as did others in his command, in which lessons were to be taught and retribution obtained.

In all of General Forrest's reports there is a "gory exultation"[101] over the consequences of the assault. On 15 April he wrote "the loss of the enemy will never be known from the fact that large numbers ran into the river and were shot and drowned. . . . The river was dyed with the blood of the slaughtered for 200 yards. There was in the fort a large number of citizens who had fled there to escape the conscript law. Most of these ran into the river and were drowned." The number of drowned citizens he estimated at over one hundred.[102] His boastful claim that he hoped the Fort Pillow affair would demonstrate to the northern people that Negro soldiers cannot cope with southerners was more than an odious racial statement. Indeed, the statement was inconsistent with his professed policy, as argued on his behalf by his friend the Reverend David C. Kelley, that Forrest did not kill black troops but preferred to return them to their owners.[103] Undoubtedly, the assertion black soldiers were inferior to Confederate soldiers could not have been made any sooner during the West Tennessee Campaign, because Forrest was turned back from Paducah. There, it will be remembered, the black troops composed approximately two fifths of the garrison. Notwithstanding their exposed positions, these troops acquitted themselves from the stereotyped slave under arms, and stayed their positions until the Confederates were driven off or retired from the field. Considering Forrest's nature, the Paducah engagement was a humiliation that could not remain unredeemed for long. Although most of the Confederates fighting at Fort Pillow had not been engaged at Paducah, the Paducah loss "undoubtedly served to intensify the fury felt by the Rebels toward Northern troops in general, and black soldiers in particular."[104]

On 15 April General Forrest also wrote to Jefferson Davis. He estimated "that in troops, negroes, and citizens the killed, wounded and drowned will range from 450 to 500." Subsequently, the number of civilian casualties would be changed to "quite a number were drowned or killed in the retreat from the fort."[105]

That Generals Forrest and Chalmers did not exercise any restraint or at no time endeavored to bring a halt to the slaughter
is contrary to testimony offered by both Federal and Confederate
witnesses. Whether this belated forbearance, however, was exer-
cised as soon as General Forrest learned of the mayhem or rather,
when he and his command sated their vengeful appetites is particularly significant to comprehending General Forrest's conscious
involvement in the affair. As previously noted, the mass of testimony has not been accumulated from Federal sources alone but
includes accusations by Forrest's own men that he ordered the
slaughter. Other, more numerous veterans of his command, wrote
in subsequent years that he acted as soon as was practical to stop
any further effusion of blood, and that he should be exonerated
from any wrongdoing. Clearly not all the Confederate troops taking part in the assault participated in the massacre. There were
reported instances where Confederate officers and men tried to
intercede and prevent the unnecessary loss of life.[106] Instances to
the contrary were more numerous.

Private Elias Falls, Company A, 6th USHA, testified killing occurred after the surrender until Forrest gave the orders to cease
and that after peace was restored some of the Confederates shot
the wounded until "an officer told the secesh soldier if he did
that again he would arrest him."[107] Duncan Harding, a private in
the same company, observed unidentified officers shouting "kill
the God damned niggers."[108] Manuel Nicholas, also a member of
the 6th United States Heavy Artillery, was wounded before the
final assault and did not go down the hill with the other troops.
After surrendering he was shot under the ear and while laying
on the ground he heard an officer call out, "Forrest says, no quarter! No quarter!" and another shout "Black flag, black flag."[109]
Francis Alexander and Alfred Coleman heard officers shouting
no quarter should be shown the Negroes and their officers.[110]
William Mays of the 13th Tennessee Cavalry claimed he heard
Confederates yelling after taking the fort "Kill'em, kill'em; God
damn'em, that's Forrest's orders, not to leave one alive."[111] Others
also swore they heard Confederates say it was Forrest's orders.[112]
Sergeant W. P. Walker claimed he heard a Confederate state it
was the order of a general, whose name he could not discern, that
all the Federals were to be shot.[113]

Dr. Fitch reported in his lengthy narrative that while he was
below the bluff he observed a group of about twenty surrendering
Federals placed in a line near the edge of the river when a volley
was fired into them bringing down all but two. General Forrest

was atop the bluff at this time sighting one of the Parrott guns on the New Era.[114] From this position, a mere hundred feet from the base of the bluff, Forrest had an unobstructed view of the incidents unfolding below him. Sergeant Benjamin Robinson testified that while he lay wounded on the hill General Forrest rode his horse over him three or four times.. General Forrest "said to some negro men there that he knew them; that they had been in his nigger yard in Memphis. He said he was not worth five dollars when he started, and had got rich trading in negroes."[115]

There are two reported instances when members of the 6th United States Heavy Artillery were shot by officers whose horses they were holding.[116] Several other episodes of officer involvement were described by survivors.[117] John Ray, Company B, 13th Tennessee Cavalry, observed General Chalmers order another officer to place on the ground a young Negro boy who was astride the junior officer's horse and shoot him or Chalmers would do it himself.[118]

Colonel Chalmers, brother of the general, informed a Federal officer the day following the battle "that he could not control his men very well, and thought [killing] was justifiable in regard to negroes; that they did not recognize negroes as soldiers, and he could not control his men."[119] General Chalmers, while accompanying several Federal officers on a field inspection of the fort the day after the battle, stated many of the Negroes were killed after they surrendered and "that the men of General Forrest's command had such a hatred toward the armed negro that they could not be restrained from killing the negroes after they had captured them." He denied the killings were the result of General Forrest's or his orders but that "Forrest and he stopped the massacre as soon as they were able to do so. He said it was nothing better than we could expect so long as we persisted in arming the negro."[120] On the same day aboard the *Platte Valley* Dr. Chapman Underwood claimed General Chalmers told him "that [Confederates] would not treat as prisoners of war the 'home-made Yankees,' meaning the loyal Tennesseans."[121]

The acting signal officer of the *New Era*, paymaster William Purdy, testified to a conversation he had with an aide to General Chalmers. "He told me that they did not recognize negroes as United States soldiers, but would shoot them, and show them no quarter—neither the negroes nor their officers. . . . He then spoke in relation to the Tennessee loyal troops. He said they did not think much of them; that they were refugees and deserters; and they would not show them much mercy either."[122] The testimony of W. R. McLagan, a conscript in the Confederate army who escaped from Forrest's command at Jackson and made his way to Memphis, is particularly revealing. On 11 April while at Covington, he overheard a conversation between Colonel Duckworth and a Captain Hill in which Duckworth remarked "that no quarter would be shown at Fort Pillow at all; that they were a set of damned Yankees and Tennessee traitors there, and they intended to show them no quarter."[123] As noted earlier fighting against one's master was an unpardonable cardinal sin and being a Yankee sympathizer was no less odious.

The Congressional Committee concluded that the incidents at Fort Pillow were not the result of the vagaries of combat "but were the results of a policy deliberately decided upon and unhesitatingly announced." Among the several items of proof weighed by the committee in reaching its conclusion were the "various demands of surrender" issued by Forrest or under his signature during the spring 1864 offensive into West Tennessee. General Brayman concurred in this assessment when he wrote in his official report that the documentation "All disclose a policy deliberately adopted, a premeditation well considered; the more than savage acts at Fort Pillow being but the natural and intended result."[124]

Confederate analysts would assuage the massacre theorists by describing these surrender demands as merely consistent with historic precedent, as previously discussed, or nothing other than documents of intimidation. General Chalmers years after the war described these demands for surrender as designed to "intimidate Forrest's adversary."[125] These ultimatums have been perceived as a "device" used "to scare the Union garrison into prompt surrender."[126] As one historian rationalized, while "Forrest was probably correct in saying that he could not be responsible for the consequences if the demand was refused," this was not the same as "ordering a slaughter."[127] These points of view project a somewhat distorted analytic perspective on the significance of the surrender demands. The considerations of historic precedent and intimidation are mutually exclusive, except when the intendment of the latter is not a veiled threat.

Although the surrender demand at Fort Pillow may have been designed to intimidate the garrison and possibly avoid the consequences of further combat, the threats hardly contained the element of posturing. Forrest was not prone to idle gestures. In the past, he had resorted to ruses in order to confuse the enemy and mislead them as to the strength and deployment of his forces. A ruse, however, is different from a threat. The statements Forrest used at Fort Pillow and sanctioned elsewhere were calculated to give warning of the dire consequences to those who would defy their "masters" or who had sullied their southern birthright by becoming renegade Tennesseans. The record amply discloses a real and personal basis for harboring resentment and the need for retaliation that was felt among the Confederate forces positioned outside the fort. Forrest's demands were a conscious appreciation of these simmering emotions among his men as well as himself, and an intentional, if not a tacit approval, of his force's anticipated reaction to any failure to surrender before the bugler sounded the charge. When a commanding general, particularly one who maintains a rigid, iron-fisted discipline over his men, refuses to accept responsibility for the anticipated behavior of his troops should surrender be refused, there is no need to order the happening of events which he acknowledges will be the natural consequence of the failure to surrender. The final communication to the garrison was not only a last appeal for surrender, but it gave approval for the reckless and wanton mischief of the attacking forces. Forrest need not have done more to produce a massacre than not issuing an order against one.[128]

In his Recollections of Fort Pillow, Captain Walter A. Goodman, adjutant-general on Chalmers staff, who was a member of the Confederate truce party, maintained he had a clear recollection of the surrender correspondence.

> [W]hen the note was handed to me, there was some discussion about it among the officers present, and it was asked whether it was intended to include the negro soldiers as well as the white; to which both general Forrest and General Chalmers replied, that it was so intended; and that if the fort was surrendered, the whole garrison, white and black, should be treated as prisoners of war. No doubt as to the meaning and scope of this proposition was ever expressed or intimated in any of the notes and conversations which followed it under the flag of truce.[129]

The argument that Forrest exonerated himself through the textual context of the surrender demand begs the issue of his anticipation and active participation in the events that befell the garrison and seeks to close the door to truth without meaningful analysis. The Confederist perception of the final surrender demand appears to champion a new theory of wrongful conduct— comparative criminality. If the victim does not cooperate with the demands of the assailant, the victim is wholly or proportionately responsible for the consequences. The history of the Civil War, with all of its barbarity, admits of only isolated instances and no formal rule of engagement that would justify the dire surrender demands issued by Forrest and his staff during their campaign into Tennessee.[130]

Were the surrender demands idle threats designed to only intimidate, General Forrest would have given explicit orders through the chain of command that needless slaughter would not be tolerated after taking the fort, and that the officers should command their troops with restraint. General Forrest not only precipitated the devastation to human life after the fort was in Confederate hands and the garrison incapable of resistance, he was a passive participant in the imbroglio, when after entering the fort he proceeded to direct the firing of a cannon at the *New Era* while Armageddon raged beneath him. A contemporary biographer, Brian Steel Wills, maintains that had Forrest intended the massacre he would have led the charge, as was his custom, wading pell mell into the fray. Curiously, this historian acknowledged Forrest may not have taken part in the charge because of injuries sustained when his horse was shot from underneath him, "or he might have sensed what was about to happen and wished to distance himself from it."[131] Forrest's fall from his horse early in the battle did cause him substantial discomfort as was evident from the period of convalescence he permitted himself at Jackson. Most certainly Forrest knew what was going to occur once his forces gained their objective. Although it was possible he sought to distance himself, more than likely he was too infirm to lead an assault over terrain that did not favor a cavalry charge before his dismounted troops scaled the parapets.

Concededly, much of the evidence against General Forrest is circumstantial and ex parte, as is similarly the case with rebuttal proof offered by Confederists. That he might escape conviction before a jury of his peers is not a vindication of his involvement or responsibility. Before the bar of history evidence is not viewed by a standard of reasonable doubt. Facts are analyzed in relation to the climate of the times, prevailing attitudes, and the probabilities inherent in known facts and circumstances. Nathan Bedford Forrest's criminality at Fort Pillow reflected behavior, whether through omission or active participation, that was encouraged and sanctioned by southern culture and Confederate law.

The conscious intention to annihilate the Federal forces at Fort Pillow may also be inferred from the information provided by Lieutenant Rawley's informant days before the attack concerning the fate of the garrison; Colonel Duckworth and Captain Hill's statement on the eve of the attack that no quarter would be shown; and Captain Goodman's clear understanding of the import of the surrender demands.

In evaluating Forrest's role in the Fort Pillow massacre, a mere recitation of the facts to proffer a particular point of view is not persuasive without considering Forrest as the man and general. Taking into account the force of his inner stirrings; the penchant for lashing out with furious and violent rage; the prior consistent behavior of his early life and military career; the obvious awareness emancipation would have upon his life; the acceptance months earlier of a cause lost; his military credo to annihilate, to slaughter no man except in combat, that if war means fighting, fighting means killing; the urgency to redress local abuses; the fire of racial antagonism; the approval inherent in CSA policy; his boastful pride in the battle's outcome; the need to redeem the loss at Paducah and prove that blacks were not the equal of Confederate soldiers, the controversy cannot seriously be pursued. The conflict within him orchestrated the tragedy at Fort Pillow.

There may not be forensic evidence or even a fingerprint left at the scene of the crime. Videotapes covering the entire engagement and confessions of wrongdoing are not available. Circumstantial evidence, though, has long been recognized as creating a clear imprint of guilt. At Fort Pillow, General Nathan Bedford Forrest left his very own imprimatur. Regardless of the absence of unequivocal proof of a direct order to massacre, the evidence ponderates with acknowledgments of Forrest's misfeasance. In failing to take effective measures to defuse or guard against the natural result of private hatreds, common fears, and vengeful feelings that animated himself as well as the men of his command, he permitted with reckless disregard, beyond all rationale, the torrents of rage to vent its malignancy upon a helpless, wounded, and beaten foe.

6

Tides of Wrath

Following his victory at Fort Pillow, General Forrest moved inland to reestablish his forces at Jackson. While passing through Brownsville, his troops were received with affectionate enthusiasm for the success his recent military operations had in West Tennessee. The people of Brownsville were confident the countryside would no longer suffer further indignities from Federal occupational forces or marauding bands of deserters and thugs. The citizenry of the town showered their hero and his staff with whatever hospitality their limited resources permitted. Forrest arrived at Jackson on the 14 April where he stayed until 2 May. There, he refitted his forces, gathered new conscripts, and nutured the injuries suffered when three of his horses were shot from under him at Fort Pillow.

The prisoners captured at Fort Pillow, numbering 226, were marched under the guard of Colonel Bell's brigade through La Grange, Tennessee, south to Holy Springs, Mississippi, and finally convoyed to Demopolis, Alabama. On 21 April, from Okolona, Mississippi, Captain John Goodwin, the provost marshall general of Forrest's cavalry department, forwarded a dispatch wherein he listed the prisoners captured at Fort Pillow. He also provided "the names and owners and residences of the negroes captured at same place."[1] The prisoner list included the names of 7 officers and 219 enlisted personnel of whom 3 officers and 55 soldiers were affiliated with either the 6th U.S. Heavy Artillery or the 2nd U.S. Light Artillery while the remainder were classified with white units.[2] Records concerning the fate of the black prisoners are either nonexistent or unreliable. Fairly accurate figures have been compiled concerning the members of Bradford's Battalion. Captain Young survived imprisonment at Cahaba, and Captain Poston escaped. Of 164 white officers and men who were marched off to prisoner of war camps, 107 died at Andersonville, 5 perished at Florence, 1 at Cahaba. One unfortunate soul, George

Kirk, survived imprisonment only to drown aboard the steamer *Gen* after she caught fire and sank off Cape Hatteras on 30 March 1865.

During spring 1866, the work of exhuming and reinternment of the Union soldiers at Fort Pillow, in a formal cemetery, was completed. The work had been ordered by the quartermaster general of the army, Major General Meigs, on 12 December 1865. "The bodies of the dead were found scattered over a wide extent of country, and were not found together in large numbers except in the immediate vicinity of the Fort. Nearly all the bodies of men who had been killed under the bluff and next to the river have been washed away by the high water during the past year."[3] Two hundred and fifty-eight bodies were recovered; only 41 of whom could be identified. With possibly 31 additional soldiers having died either enroute to Mound City aboard the steamers or while at the hospital for their wounds, this report suggests that at least 289 deaths can be confirmed. The figure does not include the number of civilian fatalities or bodies reclaimed by the river for which no accurate estimate has ever been made. Known prisoner of war deaths were also omitted.

A curious anomaly was disclosed by the commander of the burial detail. Captain Colburn described in his report that upon reliable information obtained from persons who were on the field immediately after the engagement, the body of Major Booth, previously thought to have been removed, was recovered. Eleven days after the battle, Second Lieutenant James Patrick, 2d U.S. Light Artillery (USCT), along with Captain Smith, 6th U.S. Heavy Artillery (USCT), traveled to Fort Pillow to recover the remains of members of their units who were there. They were directed, by a Confederate Major under a flag of truce, to a grave thought to contain Major Booth. Lieutenant Patrick later wrote the "body was very much swollen and mortification having taken place, it was difficult to recognize any one but from all appearances I am fully satisfied that the body in that grave at that time was the body of the late Major Booth[e], and am fully satisfied at least it was the body of a white man."[4]

The record does not indicate whether Mrs. Booth was ever aware of this possible misidentification of her husband's remains. Her immediate interest following the engagement concerned the families of the black soldiers who served with Major Booth.

Perhaps touched by the tragedy at Fort Pillow and sharing the devotion to cause and duty her husband practiced while commanding his troops, Mary Elizabeth Wayt Booth demonstrated a tender and compassionate understanding for the sorrow felt by the widows and orphans of black soldiers. Several weeks after the fall of the fort, she visited with President Lincoln to discuss the plight of the families of black servicemen. In giving her a written introduction to Senator Sumner, the president advocated her worthy platform. Senator Sumner was instrumental in passing the amendment to the army appropriation bill that finally gave equal pay status to black soldiers. She proposed "widows and children in fact, of colored soldiers who fall in our service, be placed in law, the same as if their marriages were legal, so that they can have the benefit of the provisions made the widows and orphans of white soldiers."[5] Through the efforts of Senator Sumner and other vociferous abolitionists a resolution was passed in the Senate making available to black soldiers the same pension rights enjoyed by their white comrades and accepting common law proof of cohability. The resolution made it easier for black widows to prove marriage. The bill was finally passed 2 July 1864, but not without the chilling restriction that the widows and orphans must demonstrate they were free persons. Therefore, "if a female slave in a loyal slave State had fled her bondage and 'married' a freedman legally enlisted in the Union Army . . . neither she nor her children could qualify for the pensions, being still legally slaves."[6] The injustices to pensioners were not confined to blacks. There is the incident of Captain John L. Poston, Co. E. 13th Tennessee Cavalry. He enlisted as a captain on 10 January 1864, but his company was never formally mustered into service. After being captured at Fort Pillow and escaping from Confederate prison, he served the remainder of the war as a captain in the 6th Tennessee Cavalry. After the war he suffered from diseases contracted while in captivity, but his pension claim was denied because he had not been mustered into service until after the onset of his illness.[7]

The concern for prisoners, however, was not restricted to their service benefits. Two important considerations emerged that drastically altered the status of prisoners for the remaining year of the war. During the first three years, the parties agreed to a prisoner exchange program whereby various numbers of the Union and Confederate forces held captive would be released based on a rank weighted formula. Noncommissioned officers were equal to two privates. A lieutenant was equal to four privates. A general was the equivalent of sixty privates. The excess prisoners freed would swear an oath promising they would not reenter the conflict until properly exchanged. This system of parole was honored more in the breach than in adherence to the conditions of release. As the war progressed and the resources of the South became more strained than those of its adversary, the Confederate need to reemploy parolees became proportionately greater. The disadvantage to Grant was that the Confederates captured at Vicksburg and Port Hudson for example, whose numbers aggregated some thirty-seven thousand, soon made their way to face the general again at other fronts (i.e., Chattanooga) while the reciprocal release of Federal prisoners was not forthcoming and their physical condition, for the most part, was generally unacceptable for military duty.[8]

The second concern involved the "status of colored prisoners." The war was particularly cruel to officers and men of black units captured by Confederates. Incidents of the capture and sale of blacks serving as servants in Federal units had been documented as early as February 1863. In July of the same year, General Grant endeavored to investigate the hanging of several black soldiers, a white officer, and a white sergeant after the battles of Port Hudson and Milliken's Bend. Alleged atrocities and impressment into hard labor was also rumored about the black soldiers of the 54th Massachusetts who were captured at Fort Wagner and elsewhere. Secretary of War Stanton, faced with the dilemma that the Confederates would not exchange black soldiers and their officers, sought the assistance of General Butler in formulating a more humane policy for the Federal Commissioner of Exchange. On 17 November 1863, he wrote to the general: "This is the point on which the whole matter hangs. Exchanging man for man and officer for officer, with the exception the rebels make, is a substantial abandonment of the Colored Troops and their officers to their fate, and would be a shameful dishonor to the Government bound to protect them. When they agree to exchange all alike there will be no difficulty."[9] Another six months would have to pass and the incident at Fort Pillow occur before an unequivocal policy would be put into place.

On 17 April 1864, as a result of the ongoing refusal of Confederate commanders to recognize the usual rules of war for the treatment and exchange of black servicemen and their officers taken captive and culminating with the disaster at Fort Pillow, Grant issued explicit instructions to Major General Butler. General Butler was then formally involved in negotiations for the exchange of prisoners with the Confederate commissioner for prisoners exchange, Judge Robert Ould.

No arrangement for the exchange of prisoners will be acceded to that does not fully recognize the validity of these paroles, and provide for the release to us, of a sufficient number of prisoners now held by the Confederate Authorities to cancel any balance that may be in our favor by virtue of these paroles. Until there is released to us an equal number of officers and men as were captured and paroled at Vicksburg and Port Hudson, not another Confederate prisoner of war will be paroled or exchanged.

No distinction whatever will be made in the exchange between white and colored prisoners; the only question being; were they, at the time of their capture, in the military service of the United States. If they were, the same terms as to treatment while prisoners and conditions of release and exchange must be exacted and had, in the case of colored soldiers as in the case of white soldiers.

Non-acquiescence by the Confederate Authorities in both or either of these propositions, will be regarded as a refusal on their part to agree to the further exchange of prisoners, and will be so treated by us.[10]

The effort to ameliorate the state of affairs respecting the officers and men of black units was met without success. Confederate Secretary of War Seddon, as of June 1864, was adamant as he expressed his government's policy. "I doubt, however, whether the exchange of negroes at all for our soldiers would be tolerated. As to the white officers serving with negro troops, we ought never to be inconvenienced with such prisoners."[11] Confederate commanders in the field, together with their troops, continued to exhibit an abiding hatred toward the USCT whose passionate flame could only be soothed at the point of the bayonet. Six days after the fall of Fort Pillow, at Poison Springs, Arkansas, a mixed foraging party of twelve hundred Federals were badly cut up by Confederate forces. The 79th U.S. Colored Infantry suffered 117 dead as compared to 65 wounded, an uncommon ratio of casualties for the Civil War, except when black units fell to the mercy of Confederates. Speaking of the incident, a Federal colonel charged "I have the most positive assurances from eye-witnesses that they were murdered on the spot."[12] On 25 April at Mark's Mill a member of Shelby's division described the battlefield as "sickening to behold. No orders, threats, or commands could restrain the men from vengeance on the negroes, and they were piled in great heaps about the wagons, in the tangled brushwood, and upon the muddy and trampled road."[13] Along the North Carolina coast at Plymouth, also in April 1864, more atrocities would be committed. A Union sergeant wrote:

All the negroes found in blue uniforms or with any outward marks of a Union soldier upon him were killed—I saw some taken into the woods and hung—others I saw stripped of all their clothing, and they stood along the bank of the river with their faces riverwards and then they were shot—still others were killed by having their brains beaten out by the butt end of the muskets in the hands of the rebels. All were not killed the day of the capture. Those that were not were placed in a room with their officers, they [the officers] having previously been dragged through the town with ropes around their necks, where they were kept confined until the following morning when the remainder of the black soldiers were killed.[14]

At Saltville, Virginia, in October 1864 the Confederates were initially driven from their trenches. Shortly after the Federals were similarly repulsed, blacks taken prisoner were killed, and seven others lying wounded in hospitals were executed.[15]

The unfavorable treatment accorded black servicemen and their officers was not confined to Confederate troops. Confederate citizens and partisans surrounded a foraging party of twenty men from the 51st U.S. Colored Infantry. After forcing them to surrender, they murdered and mutilated the enlisted men, shooting their lieutenant through the mouth. In Kentucky, guerrillas attacked a detachment of ten men from the 108th U.S. Colored Infantry, killing three and butchering their bodies. In Georgia, several weeks later, guerrillas killed three black troops from the 40th U.S. Colored Infantry, splitting their heads with an ax.[16]

The barbarity practiced by some Confederate troops had no meaningful impact upon the southern war effort. Indeed, these atrocities only strengthened the resolve of black units to fight harder and with a more determined resolve to defeat their enemies. In due course, the tides of wrath would reverse their/course and, with an equanimity of measured violence, wreck havoc upon an opposite shore. As Sherman predicted, retaliation would become a device in the hands of the ordinary soldier made desperate by the warfare of a vengeful foe. Perhaps from an acceptance of the black soldier's tenacity and valor in battle, or an understanding and respect that emerges as association whittles away the barriers of prejudice, or out of an abiding sense of fealty borne from suffering under a common banner, retaliation would find equal expression among whites as among black Federal troops. Several weeks after the battle a white officer in the 68th U.S. Colored Infantry recorded the reaction of his troops as they passed Fort Pillow. "The motto of the 68th is, 'Remember Fort Pillow' and from the grim faces that gazed so intently today, upon that silent bluff, and the fierce threats that were passed around, I know that Fort Pillow will be held in remembrance when the 68th comes to show mercy."[17] In Memphis the black troops took an oath on bended knee to show no quarter and avenge the atrocities at Fort Pillow. Clearly, summary executions of prisoners, brutalization of wounded, and assorted acts of barbarity was not the private domain of one side, but something at which two could play.[18]

A USCT officer described that after trapping ten Confederates his troops gunned down five. "Had it not been for Ft. Pillow", he wrote his wife, "those 5 men might be alive now, 'Remember Fort Pillow' is getting to be the feeling if not the word. It looks hard but we cannot blame these men much." In Louisiana, a company of black cavalrymen, being encouraged by their officer to "Remember Fort Pillow," captured and executed seventeen guerrilla prisoners. A Confederate general complained that one of his privates captured by the 26th U.S. Colored Infantry had been bayoneted six or seven times. A Maine cavalryman informed a friend he witnessed black troops executing Confederates after they surrendered. The unit involved was the same regiment who observed some of their comrades hanged outside the fortress walls of Port Hudson after that unsuccessful attack. At Fort Blakely, Alabama, after the blacks attacked, "the rebs were panic-struck. Numbers of them jumped into the river and were drowned attempting to cross, or were shot while swimming. Still others threw down their arms and ran for their lives over to the white troops on our left, to give themselves up, to save being butchered." The officer who wrote this account was not in the Confederate service at Fort Pillow, but a lieutenant in the USCT. The threat of "No quarter" was a double-edged sword that could cut both ways.[19]

While on board a steamer in the Yazoo River, a civilian told a major and several of his officers that General Forrest was correct for having massacred the blacks at Fort Pillow. Still later, the same individual threatened a black sentinel with deadly physical harm. As if this was not enough, the civilian was making money in cotton speculation, the very commodity being guarded by the black troops aboard the boat. A rump trial was presided over by twenty-one officers, and the civilian was convicted of a death threat to a Federal officer and hanged. Notwithstanding the protestations of superiors, the regimental commander supported his officers and the men were retained in the service.[20]

At Jenkins Ferry in Arkansas on 30 April, the 2nd Kansas Colored, an affiliate regiment of the 79th Infantry that was mauled at Poison Springs, vowed to take no prisoners. After fighting for two hours, the troops were being hammered by a Confederate battery. They successfully stormed the three guns shouting "Remember Poison Spring." The Confederate killed totaled 150 whereas the 2nd Kansas Colored lost only 15 men killed and 55 others wounded.[21]

An Iowa unit affiliated with Sherman's army boasted of killing twenty-three prisoners after first reminding the victims of Fort Pillow. "When there is no officer with us we take no prisoners. We want revenge," a Wisconsin volunteer admitted.[22]

At the Battle of Resaca, Georgia, in May 1864, members of the 105th Illinois, part of the Third Division, 20th Army, under General Hooker and attached to Sherman's army, successfully stormed a Confederate battery at Buzzard's Roost. Cowering under one of the gun carriages was a Confederate who had tattooed on his arm "Fort Pillow." His captors set upon him instantly, yelling "No quarter for you!" bayoneting and shooting him numerous times.[23]

Colonel Thomas J. Morgan's description of his fighting units gives credence to the fact that Fort Pillow only served to reinforce the resolve of Federal troops. The colonel commanded a brigade of four black regiments. At Pulaski, Tennessee, on 27 September 1864 his troops, reinforcing General Rousseau, came up against General Forrest's forces.

The massacre of colored troops at Fort Pillow was well known to us, and had been fully discussed by our men. It was rumored, and thoroughly credited by them, that General Forest had offered a thousand dollars for the head of any commander of a "nigger regiment." Here, then, was just such an opportunity as those spoiling for a fight might desire. Negro troops stood face to face with Forest's veteran cavalry. The fire was growing hotter, and balls were uncomfortably thick. At length, the enemy in strong force, with banners flying, bore down toward us in full sight, apparently bent on mischief. Pointing to the advancing column, I said, as I passed along the line, "Boys, it looks very much like fight; keep cool, do your duty." They seemed full of glee, and replied with great enthusiasm: "Colonel, dey can't whip us, dey nebber get de ole 14th out of heah, nebber." "Nebber drives us away widout a mighty lot of dead men," &c., &c.

When Forrest learned that Rousseau was re-enforced by infantry, he did not stop to ask the color of their skin, but after testing their line, and finding it unyielding, turned to the east, and struck over toward Murfreesboro.[24]

An officer assigned to a Black regiment affiliated with the Army of the Potomac wrote in May 1864, "the rebels will not stand against our colored soldiers when there is any chance of them being taken prisoners, for they are conscious of what they justly deserve. Our men went into these works after they were taken, yelling, 'Fort Pillow!'" This officer surmised the enemy had already lost two for every one they "inhumanly murdered."[25]

A soldier fighting with a white unit in the trenches outside Petersburg wrote the black troops refuse to take prisoners, and their cry is "Remember Fort Pillow."[26]

Unphased by the torrents of rage he unleashed or the horrid consequences that would surely follow, Forrest pushed on. After leaving Jackson, he would continue the war effort with unabated aggressiveness and ferocity. Months earlier he knew the Confederate cause was in its death throes, but he would not shirk from his military responsibility. The war certainly was not showing signs of winding down despite his objective assessment for its outcome. Ahead were to be fought some of the most desperate and savage engagements yet witnessed. The Wilderness, Sherman's capture of Atlanta and March to the Sea, the Bloody Angle at Spotsylvania, Kinesaw Mountain, Cold Harbor, the Crater, Fort Steadman, the Seige of Petersburg, and Cedar Creek would reach new heights of human suffering; gory reenactments of tens of thousands of Cains venting their anger on an equal number of Abels. The fields one day would be marked by the obelisks, statuary, and plaques typically reflective of mournful remembrances and a national consciousness of guilt. But, it was still spring 1864, and in Forrest's military department there was much hate.

General Sturgis, on 31 May, set out from Memphis, with a force of 8,300 troops, 22 cannons, and 250 wagons in pursuit of Forrest. General Grierson led the cavalry, and General McMillen's infantry consisted of 1,200 black troops under the command of Colonel Edward Bouton. Five days later a foray of 400 troops would destroy bridges and railroad trestles at Rienzi, Mississippi. With a "sad foreboding of the consequences,"[27] Sturgis would push on to Tupelo where Forrest's forces were believed to be located. Forrest would not wait for him there, but chose instead a place known as Brice's Cross Roads or Tishomingo Creek. Early in the morning on 10 June, advance elements of dismounted cavalry began skirmishing, which became quite severe by one o'clock. The Federal infantry started out late that morning and were hampered by the endless stream of wagons encumbering the line of march. At about twelve o'clock, the main body of troops were still five miles from the crossroads. The Federals engaged were drawn up in a defensive, semicircle position, being pressed on all sides. The reinforcements were called up and quick marched the five miles in oppressively hot weather.

In characteristic fashion, Forrest sent one of Buford's regiments to the enemy's left rear and Buford himself on the right. The attack was dogged until five o'clock when the Federal lines broke and a route of uncontrollable proportions engulfed the troops. The situation became more desperate when wagons attempting to recross the creek on the only bridge available became congested. Caissons, wagons, and ambulances vied with the retreating troops to escape the chaos that enveloped the battlefield. In the stampede, wagons were abandoned and burned. Guns were left behind where they had become stuck in the quagmire. New defensive lines were quickly forced to pull back as darkness settled upon the scene, Forrest sent small detachments to continue harassing the Federals as the main body of Confederates rested and consumed the spoils of their victory. The retreat was marked by complete disorder that was repeated the next day at the prodding of Forrest's pursuing forces.

The Federals required nine days to march from outside Memphis to Brice's Cross Roads but only two nights and a day to retrace the same fifty-eight miles. Sturgis reported 223 killed and 394 wounded; Confederate losses were estimated at 96 killed and 396 wounded.[28] The real difference was not the casualties. Some 1,600 Federals were taken prisoner, whereas no Confederates were captured. With a force of 5,000, Forrest routed over 8,000 Federals and captured 16 serviceable guns, 1,500 small arms, huge quantities of ordinance, 176 wagons, and assorted other supplies and equipment.

Despite Bouton's Colored Infantry Brigade, the 59th Colored Regiment, and the 4th Iowa putting up a respectable rear action, the battle was lost and Sturgis soundly whipped by the Confederates. General Sturgis's overconfident boasting and the piecemeal misuse of his troops in unfavorable climate and terrain sealed the battle's outcome. The black brigade suffered as many wounded as any other brigade, but as many killed as suffered by the combined five brigades.[29] Chagrined at the Sturgis disaster, Sherman wrote he would make up a new force to "follow Forrest to the death if it costs 10,000 lives and breaks the Treasury. There never will be peace in Tennessee until Forrest is dead."[30]

Forrest succeeded in frustrating his nemesis Sherman whose attempts to dragoon the elusive general usually met either with defeat or unsatisfactory results. Not only was Sherman willing to figuratively expend ten thousand lives and bankrupt the national treasury to rid the field of "that devil Forrest," but on 24 June 1864, he proposed to President Lincoln another alternative. "I have ordered General A. J. Smith and General Mower to pursue and kill Forrest, promising the latter, in case of success, my influence to promote him to Major General. He is one of the gamest men in our service. Should accident befall me, I ask you to favor him, if he succeeds in killing Forrest."[31]

During the late summer of 1864, General Forrest put into motion one of his most daring raids of the war. After having taken a circuitous route through the familiar surroundings of Hernando, Mississippi, wading through oppressive mud roads and fording swollen streams with makeshift pontoon bridges, he arrived on Sunday, 21 August, outside of Memphis. Detailed and precise orders were directed to the various commanders who would have a special role to play. Chalmers was directed to make a strong diversionary demonstration in front of the Federals while Forrest and fifteen hundred troops would seek out their special quarries. Captain Forrest moved out toward the forward sentries as the faint rays of the morning sun began to rise. Although he succeeded in surprising this first group of defenders a reserve picket further up the road was able to sound the alarm. The remaining Confederates were ordered forward at once. Three Union generals were the sought-after prizes: Washburn, Hurlbut, and Burckland.

Captain Forrest proceeded with all celerity to the Gayoso House where Major General Stephen Hurlbut and his staff were reported quartered. Major General Cadwallader Washburn, who made his headquarters in a house on Union Street, was the target of another of General Forrest's brothers, Colonel Jesse Forrest. Upon arriving at the Gayoso House, the Confederates rushed in on horseback only to learn that Hurlbut had slept elsewhere that evening. Awakened by the alarm of an orderly sent to arouse him, General Washburn retreated in all haste to the safety of Fort Pickering clad only in his cutty sark or "nocturnal habiliments," leaving his uniform and accessories as a spoil of war.

General Burckland, also aroused by a diligent sentry, sought refuge in another building. A strong defense was hastily organized by directing Federals to a brick building. With the militia having rallied to the alarm and the Federals establishing strong lines, the Confederates proceeded to withdraw under the bugler's sound of recall.

As the Confederates poured out of Memphis, their rear guard

was attacked by a detachment of cavalry under the command of Colonel Starr, the officer who aroused General Washburn. With his escort, General Forrest made a countercharge, driving off the Federals and personally causing serious injury to Colonel Starr. Hours later, another column of six hundred cavalry was sent in pursuit, but they were delayed by a flag of truce and limited rations.

General Washburn's uniform would be returned, and the general would extend the courtesy by sending General Forrest a uniform specially made for him by a Memphis tailor.

General Forrest reported, "I attacked Memphis at four o'clock this morning, driving the enemy to his fortifications. We killed or captured four hundred (later paroling the prisoners), taking their entire camp, with about three hundred horses and mules. Washburn and staff escaped in the darkness of the early morning, Washburn leaving his clothes behind."[32]

Years later, General Chalmers would attribute to General Hurlbut the quip "They removed me from command because I couldn't keep Forrest out of West Tennessee, but Washburn couldn't keep him out of his bedroom."[33]

A Federal grand jury was convened in Memphis, and an arrest warrant issued for General Forrest on 4 September 1864. He was charged with treason for having disavowed his "allegiance and fidelity" to the United States and "intending by all the means in his power to aid and assist the persons exercising the powers of Government in the said The Confederate States of America" did aid in the insurrection "with a great Multitude of persons" whose names were unknown to the Grand Jury, but who were "armed and amassed in a warlike manner" and assaulted Memphis. The Federal marshall could not, of course, execute the arrest warrant during hostilities. After the war, Forrest appeared voluntarily before the Federal District Court of West Tennessee and, on 13 March 1866, posted a $10,000 bond. No further action was ever taken against him, and the charges were never formally withdrawn or dismissed.[34] Forrest did eventually receive a pardon from President Johnson on 17 July 1868.

By the fall, Forrest had proceeded northeast to the Tennessee River. The river was a major lifeline for providing General Sherman with most of the supplies, equipment, material, ammunition, forage, and food required of his huge army as it moved through Georgia. As the army advanced further away from its base of supplies, the protection along this lifeline became less effective and the route of transport more vulnerable to attack. This is precisely what happened on 3 November at Johnsonville, Tennessee. Johnsonville was a large depot for loading vessels heading south to replenish the needs of Sherman's army. The depot was located twenty-five miles south of Fort Heiman and was protected by a fortified garrison and numerous tin clads or gun boats.

Despite having captured two gun boats on the river on 28 October, no effort was mounted to dislodge Forrest from his proximity to Johnsonville. On 3 November, he opened an effective artillery bombardment upon the depot. This firing was substantially immune from Federal counterfire. When the cannonading had ceased, Forrest had destroyed enormous quantities of stores and set fire to numerous buildings and barges. The attack destroyed 5 gun boats, 14 transports, 18 barges, 32 guns, netted 150 prisoners, and ruined 75 tons of assorted supplies valued at $8 million.

General Sherman, with an obviously restrained annoyance, wrote General Grant "that Devil Forrest was down and about Johnsonville and making havoc among the gunboats and transports."

As spring again renewed the promise of life, there would be one more major battle to be fought by General Forrest. The battle for Selma, Alabama, would conclude General Forrest's military career. The successes he enjoyed in most prior engagements would elude him on this last occasion.

On 22 March 1865, Major General James Harrison Wilson, a protege of Generals Grant and Sheridan, had assembled a force of over thirteen thousand men and three batteries of artillery on the south shore of the Tennessee River in the northwest corner of Alabama. His cavalry force of twelve thousand five hundred mounted troopers were armed with Spencer repeating rifles and well led. They would set out this day for Selma, 160 miles south in central Alabama. Selma was an industrial center situated on the Alabama River. Destruction of its arsenals, railroad yards, and machine shops was an important military objective for the Federals. By 30 March, General Wilson's troops had crossed the Cahaba River near Elyton (Birmingham) some 120 miles from their point of embarkation. The following day, this aggressive West Point graduate and competent cavalryman had succeeded in deploying his advance elements approximately 50 miles north of Selma at Montevallo.

During this same period, Forrest had been endeavoring to bring together his widely scattered forces of seven to eight thousand to protect Selma. The Federals swept through Montevallo and on the evening of 31 March, after overcoming stubborn Confederate resistance, were outside Randolph, several miles closer to their objective. Of major significance this day would be Wilson's interception of a Confederate courier who carried two dispatches describing the location of some of Forrest's troops. With this knowledge, Wilson was able to effectively separate Forrest from three thousand of his troops by burning a bridge at Centreville and, in addition, placing brigades so as to effectively deny Forrest the opportunity to strike Wilson's right flank. On 1 April, the Federal advance was renewed, and Forrest chose a spot twenty-five miles north of Selma near the Ebenezer Baptist Church, several miles north of Plantersville, to face down the Federals. Before the day ended, there occurred one of the fiercest hand-to-hand conflicts among cavalry during the Civil War. Forrest notched his twenty-ninth combat kill and suffered his fourth wound. The Confederates, outnumbered three to one, were driven from the field. Chalmers's three thousand troops could not reach Forrest in time, and Jackson's force of three thousand was cut off. The Federals hounded Forrest to Selma where in the late afternoon of 2 April a better informed General Wilson overran the trenches and again drove Forrest from the field. The war ended within several weeks, and Forrest closed his military career with this defeat. Time had finally caught up with Forrest although it could never erase his successes and the deep abiding confidence of his men and the respect of his enemies. He disbanded his cavalry on 9 May, never formally surrendering his forces to the Federal government.

The rebellion had come to a close but for many the war lingered like a festering sore. Eventually, the wounds of the nation would heal, the enmities between sides vanish, and the nation would rise again with a singleness of voice that would not, however, echo a wholesomeness of harmony and equality. Forrest would return to his family's plantation at Sunflower Landing, Coahoma County, Mississippi. In an effort to rebuild his life and recover his wealth, Forrest tried his hand at a number of ventures but farming and later railroad building were to be his main vocations. Reconstruction created new political problems for returning Confederates, and petty vendettas prevented the full restoration of peace. In this context, which is a more complicated circumstance than can be properly treated here, a need arose for vigilante justice and the protection of Confederate veterans and their families from persecution and abuse.

The Klu Klux Klan originated in Tennessee as a means of confronting these political and social threats. One of the founding patriarchs was Nathan Bedford Forrest. The accolade of Wizard of the Saddle would be exchanged for the mantle of Grand Wizard of the Invisible Empire, and his followers would ride hooded into the night behind the sheets of a cowardly bravado. To be sure, the Klan's original agenda was not restricted to racial antagonism, as political considerations motivated them as well. Forrest's affiliation with the Klan, however, was short-lived. Either because he accepted the futility of further conflict or was motivated by the self-serving interests of ill health, an open Federal indictment, and not wanting to jeopardize his presidential pardon, he disbanded his klavern in 1869.[35]

Forrest rebuilt his plantation and expanded his other interests. He never attained his prior level of wealth and on 29 October 1877, at the age of fifty-six, he died after a long illness of chronic dysentery.

In Forrest Park, outside the campus of the University of Memphis, a handsome equestrian statue, depicting General Forrest astride his horse, King Philip, casts an imposing appearance. Beneath the base lay the remains of General Forrest and his wife, Mary Montgomery. Etched in its stone pedestal is an inscription by Virginia Frazer Boyle, "Those hoofbeats did not die upon fame's crimsoned sod. But will ring through her song and her story: He fought like a Titan and struck like a God, and his dust is our ashes of glory." While for some his dust became ashes of glory, for others his dust ignited the glorious flame of freedom.

Whether as a result of the Fort Pillow incident and other similarly reported atrocities or out of their own very personal commitment to social justice, blacks enlisted in greater numbers during the last year of the war. U.S. Colored troops participated in all the major engagements during this period with the exception of Sherman's invasion of Georgia. By October 1864, there were 140 black regiments of nearly 102,000 soldiers.[36] Their numbers swelled to more than 123,000 in 120 infantry regiments, 12 heavy artillery regiments, 10 light artillery regiments, and 7 cavalry regiments by 15 July, 1865. Approximately 180,000 served throughout the war, and together with their 7,125 white officers, they comprised 9–10 percent of the aggregate Union forces. In combat, 2,751 were killed and 34,100 died from wounds and disease. With total African American deaths totaling about 68,000, the mortality rate from all causes per thousand was greater among blacks than in white units.[37] Despite the testament to their valor covering the now muted battlements and fields of Fort Wagner, Fort Pillow, Port Hudson, Milliken's Bend, Olustee, Big Black

Forrest Statue in Memphis.

River, the Crater, New Market Heights, Petersburg, Chaffin's Farm, Nashville, Fair Oaks, and Dalton, no monument has ever been erected to commemorate a grateful nation's remembrance for the role they and their officers played in preserving the Union.

After the battle of Nashville, Colonel Thomas J. Morgan described the black soldier's contribution most eloquently.

> Colored soldiers had fought side by side with white troops. They had mingled together in the charge. They had supported each other. They had assisted each other from the field when wounded, and they lay side by side in death. The survivors rejoiced together over a hard-fought field, won by common valor. All who witnessed their conduct gave them equal praise. The day we longed to see had come and gone, and the sun went down upon a record of coolness, bravery, manliness,

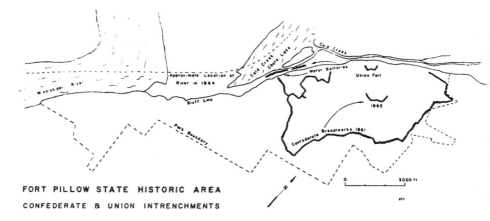

FORT PILLOW STATE HISTORIC AREA

CONFEDERATE & UNION INTRENCHMENTS

Fort Pillow State Historic Area, 1993. Appeared in *Archaeological Investigations at Fort Pillow State Historic Area, 1976–1978.*

never to be unmade. A new chapter in the history of liberty had been written. It had been shown that marching under the flag of freedom, animated by a love of liberty, even the slave becomes a man and a hero.[38]

Today, Fort Pillow remains high atop Chickasaw Bluff, its earthwork restored and the approach from the river side still marked by an escarpment. The river no longer passes beneath the bluff but has moved northwest about a mile. A new stand of forest has grown up to reclaim the cleared land encroaching within several yards of the outer parapet's ditch. Much of the land is etched by the deep scars of constant erosion. The serpentine entrenchments enveloping the fort's outer perimeter have been worn by the elements to rounded mounds of their former appearance. The wooded area outside the main fortification is dotted with grassy knolls, camp sites, a playground, picnic spots, and lakes for fishing. This sylvan setting no longer bears any traces of the numerous buildings and barracks that comprised the camp and town. Precipitous sloped hillocks continue to characterize the region with deep gullies winding an almost endless labyrinth between the hills and ridges.

The capcophony of rifle and cannon fire and the shouts and screams of the combatants have longed ceased their mournful echo through the gullies and across the hills. The rains of 128 years have cleansed the soil of the stained reminders of a bloodied and tragic conflict. The traces of combat and the mementos of camp life have long been recovered or remain secreted in earth's bosom. What does remain are the immutable facts, like a bastion, repelling the onslaught of contrived analysis and misleading details.

General Forrest may well have earned the adoration and esteem of his followers. The ledger of his victors, the quality of his leadership, his innovative tactics, the untutored genius he demonstrated in combat are signal measurements of a successful military career. Undoubtedly, the experiences of his early life and the eruptive nature of his personality influenced his conduct in war. While revered for his military greatness, he exemplified the consumate racist fighting in a race war. He was the product of a society that measured its worth upon the toil of others and fought and died to preserve the right to choose to deny others the right of choice. Forrest intended a massacre at Fort Pillow because he was obeying the higher law of a government that encouraged and sanctioned such barbarity. He echoed the ideals of a society that could not tolerate civil rights for all persons, but would champion a cause that condemned a class of people to eternal oppression. To maintain he and his troops did not intend to slaughter the garrison and that a massacre, if it occurred, resulted from the garrison's own folly is to give succor to the principles of a cause that has long ago lost the battle with common decency and nobler ideals.

War by its very nature encompasses a wickedness that is inherently barbarous. The real spoils of war are found in the savage slaughter of armed conflict that leaves its hallmark on battlefields strewn with human debris rather than the trinkets and other possessions scavenged from abandoned camps or plundered from captured wagon trains and sutler stores. Despite war's cruelty, the tacit understanding among military leaders and the rules of engagement are not without some semblance of civility.

The battle of Fort Pillow was devoid of the customary and acceptable rules of warfare then existing. The result was indeed an intentional massacre—an occurrence that was ordained by the events of an increasingly brutal and desperate war that preceded the occurrence. The event was equally influenced by the nature of the general who conceived the assault and who epitomized all the evil inherent in a society determined to preserve the pernicious institution of slavery. There are fewer inconsistencies in the record than there are recollections of fixed moments from different prospectives. That Dr. Fitch or others were protected by Confederate officers does not negate the testimony of those who saw or heard the involvement of other officers. That some would state they were given warning to get out of buildings to be set ablaze or did not see the hospital facility they were in set on fire is hardly proof other contrary accounts were fabricated. That one Federal soldier erroneously identified General Forrest as "a little bit of a man" who was observed in the fort ordering the killings, does not cast doubt upon the reliability of other Federal and Confederate accounts that the rebels were carrying out Forrest's orders.[39] The wreakage of the aftermath, the actual proof of human suffering, the uncommon nature of the casualties, the accounts and admissions of participants, the festering hatred precipitating the attack, and a publicly proclaimed Confederate government policy that sanctioned such deeds provides unimpeachable testament to the truth that an intentional massacre occurred.

Confederists who would acquit General Forrest of any wrongdoing are inclined to idolize him with an almost fictional quality. They are too firmly ensconced at the statue of adulation to ever permit history to judge Forrest unfavorably. History, however, does not judge or choose sides. Within the arena of historical debate, the scholar bears the responsibility to objectively assimilate and interpret the available data. Through the tiresome maze of source materials one must be prepared to accept unpopular and unanticipated conclusions; conclusions that are nevertheless supported by empirical wisdom. Through this process of research we learn history's profitable lesson, that while truth may not always be palatable, truth is immortal. From the lines of Maya Angelou's inspirational verse *On the Pulse of Morning*, we are reminded that "history, despite its wrenching pain, cannot be unlived, and if faced with courage, need not be lived again."

Appendix

Report of the Sub-Committee of the Joint Committee on the Conduct and Expenditures of the War

Mr. Wade submitted the following REPORT

The Joint Committee on the Conduct and Expenditures of the War, to whom was referred the resolution of Congress instructing them to investigage the late massacre at Fort Pillow, designated two members of the committee—Messrs. Wade and Gooch—to proceed forthwith to such places as they might deem necessary, and take testimony. That sub-committee having discharged that duty, returned to this city, and submitted to the joint committee a report, with accompanying papers and testimony. The report was read and adopted by the committee, whose chairman was instructed to submit the same, with the testimony, to the Senate, and ask that the same be printed.

REPORT OF THE SUB-COMMITTEE

Messrs. Wade and Gooch, the sub-committee appointed by the Joint Committee on the Conduct and Expenditures of the War, with instructions to proceed to such points as they might deem necessary for the purpose of taking testimony in regard to the massacre at Fort Pillow, submitted the following report to the joint committee, together with the accompanying testimony and papers.

In obedience to the instructions of this joint committee adopted on the 18th ultimo, your committee left Washington on the morning of the 19th, taking with them the stenographer of this committee, and proceeded to Cairo and Mound City, Illinois; Columbus, Kentucky; and Fort Pillow and Memphis, Tennessee; at each of which places they proceeded to take testimony.

Although your committee were instructed to inquire only in reference to the attack, capture and massacre of Fort Pillow, they have deemed it proper to take some testimony in reference to the operations of Forrest and his command immediately preceding and subsequent to that horrible transaction. It will appear, from the testimony thus taken, that the atrocities committed at Fort Pillow were not the result of passions excited by the heat of conflict, but were the results of a policy deliberately decided upon and unhesitatingly announced. Even if the uncertainty of

159

the fate of those officers and men belonging to colored regiments who have heretofore been taken prisoners by the rebels has failed to convince the authorities of our government of this fact, the testimony herewith submitted must convince even the most skeptical that it is the intention of the rebel authorities not to recognize the officers and men of our colored regiments as entitled to the treatment accorded by all civilized nations to prisoners of war. The declarations of Forrest and his officers, both before and after the capture of Fort Pillow, as testified by such of our men as have escaped after being taken by him; the threats contained in the various demands for surrender made at Paducah, Columbus, and other places; the renewal of the massacre the morning after the capture of Fort Pillow; the statements made by the rebel officers to the officers of our gunboats, who received the few survivors at Fort Pillow—all this proves most conclusively the policy they have determined to adopt. The first operation of any importance was the attack upon Union City, Tennessee, by a portion of Forrest's command. The attack was made on the 24th of March. The post was occupied by a force of about 500 men under Colonel Hawkins, of the 7th Tennessee Union cavalry. The attacking force was superior in numbers, but was repulsed several times by our force. For the particulars of the attack, and the circumstances attending the surrender, your committee would refer to the testimony herewith submitted. They would state, however, that it would appear from the testimony that the surrender was opposed by nearly if not quite all the officers of Colonel Hawk's command. Your committee think that the circumstances connected with the surrender are such that they demand the most searching investigation by the military authorities, as, at the time of the surrender, but one man on our side had been injured.

On the 25th of March, the enemy, under the rebel Generals Forrest, Buford, Harris and Thompson, estimated at over 6,000 men, made an attack on Paducah, Kentucky, which post was occupied by Colonel S. G. Hicks, 40th Illinois regiment, with 655 men. Our forces retired into Fort Anderson, and there made their stand—assisted by some gunboats belonging to the command of Captain Shirk of the navy—successfully repelling the attacks of the enemy. Failing to make an impression upon our forces, Forrest then demanded an unconditional surrender, closing his communication to Colonel Hicks in these words: "If you surrender you shall be treated as prisoners of war, but if I have to storm your works you may expect no quarter." This demand and threat was met by a refusal on the part of Colonel Hicks to surrender, he stating that he had been placed there by his government to defend that post, and he should do so. The rebels made three other assaults that same day, but were repulsed with heavy loss each time, the rebel General Thompson being killed in the last assault. The enemy retired the next day, having suffered a loss estimated at three hundred killed, and from 1,000 to 1,200 wounded. The loss on our side was 14 killed and 46 wounded.

The operations of the enemy at Paducah were characterized by the same bad faith and treachery that seem to have become the settled policy of Forrest and his command. The flag of truce was taken advantage of there, as elsewhere, to seecure desirable positions which the rebels were unable to obtain by fair and honorable means; and also to afford opportunities for plundering private stores as well as government property. At Paducah the rebels were guilty of acts more cowardly, if possible, than any have practiced elsewhere. When the attack was made the officers of the fort and of the gunboats advised the women and children to go down to the river for the purpose of being taken across out of danger. As they were leaving the town for that purpose, the rebel sharpshooters mingled with them, and, shielded by their presence, advanced and fired upon the gunboats, wounding some of our officers and men. Our forces could not return the fire without endangering the lives of the women and children. The rebels also placed women in front of their lines as they moved on the fort, or were proceeding to take positions while the flag of truce was at the fort, in order to compel our men to withhold their fire, out of regard for the lives of the women who were made use of in this most cowardly manner. For more full details of the attack, and the treacherous and cowardly practices of the rebels there, your committee refer to the testimony herewith submitted.

On the 13th of April, the day after the capture of Fort Pillow, the rebel General Buford appeared before Columbus, Kentucky, and demanded its unconditional surrender. He coupled with that demand a threat that if the place was not surrendered, and he should be compelled to attack it, "no quarter whatever would be shown to the negro troops." To this colonel Lawrence, in command of the Post, replied, that "surrender was out of the question," as he had been placed there by his government to hold and defend the place, and should do so. No attack was made, but the enemy retired, having taken advantage of the flag of truce to seize some horses of Union citizens which had been brought in there for security.

It was at Fort Pillow, however, that the brutality and cruelty of the rebels were most fearfully exhibited. The garrison there, according to the last returns received at headquarters, amounted to 19 officers and 538 enlisted men, of whom 262 were colored troops, comprising one battalion of the 6th United States heavy artillery, (formerly called the 1st Alabama artillery,) of colored troops, under command of Major L. F. Booth; one section of the 2d United States light artillery, colored, and one battalion of the 13th Tennessee cavalry, white, commanded by Major W. F. Bradford. Major Booth was the ranking officer, and was in command of the post. On Tuesday, the 12th of April, (the anniversary of the attack of Fort Sumter, in April, 1861) the pickets of the garrison were driven in just before sunrise, that being the first intimation our forces there had of any intention on the part of the enemy to attack that place. Fighting soon became general, and about 9 o'clock Major Booth was killed. Major Bradford succeeded to the command, and withdrew all the forces within the fort; they had previously occupied some intrenchments at some distance from the fort, and further from the river.

This fort was situated on a high bluff on the river side being covered with trees, bushes and fallen timber. Extending back from the river, on either side of the fort, as a ravine or hollow—the one below the fort containing several private stores and some dwellings, constituting what was called the town. At the mouth of that ravine, and on the river bank, were some government buildings containing commissary and quartermaster's stores. The ravine above the fort was known as Cold Creek ravine, the sides being covered with trees and bushes. To the right, or below and a little to the front of the fort, was a level piece of ground, not quite so elevated as the fort itself, on which had been erected some log huts or shanties, which were occupied by the white troops, and also used for hospital and other purposes. Within the fort tents had been erected, with board floors, for the use of the colored troops. There were six pieces of artillery in the fort, consisting of two 6-pounders, two 12 pounder howitzers and two 10 pounder Parrotts. The rebels continued their attack, but, up to two or three o'clock in the afternoon, they had not gained any decisive success. Our troops, both white and black, fought most bravely, and were in good spirits. The gunboat No. 7, (New Era,) Captain Marshall, took part in the conflict, shelling the enemy as opportunity offered. Signals had been agreed upon by which the officers in the fort could indicate where the guns of the boat could be most effective. There being but one gunboat there, no permanent impression appears to have been produced upon the enemy; for as they were shelled out of one ravine, they would make their appearance in the other. They would thus appear and retire as the gunboat moved from one point to the other. About one o'clock the fire on both sides slackened somewhat, and the gunboat moved out in the river, to cool and clean its guns, having fired 282 rounds of shell, shrapnel, and canister, which nearly exhausted its supply of ammunition. The rebels having thus far failed in their attack, now resorted to their customary use of flags of truce. The first flag of truce conveyed a demand from Forrest for the unconditional surrender of the fort. To this Major Bradford replied, asking to be allowed one hour to consult with his officers and the officers of the gunboat. In a short time a second flag of truce appeared, with a communication from Forrest, that he would allow Major Bradford twenty minutes in which to move his troops out of the fort, and if it was not done within that time an assault would be ordered. To this Major Bradford returned the reply that he would not surrender.

During the time these flags of truce were flying, the rebels were moving down the ravine and taking positions from which the more readily to charge upon the fort. Parties of them were also engaged in plundering the government buildings of commissary and quartermaster's stores, in full view of the gunboat. Captain Marshall states that he refrained from firing upon the rebels, although they were thus violating the flag of truce, for fear that, should they finally succeed in capturing the fort, they would justify any atrocities they might commit by saying that they were in retaliation for his firing while the flag of truce was flying. He says, however, that when he saw the rebels coming down the ravine above the fort, and taking positions there, he got under way and stood for the fort, determined to use what little ammunition he had left in shelling them out of the ravine, but did not get up within effective range before the final assault was made. Immediately after the second flag of truce retired, the rebels made a rush from the positions they had so treacherously gained and obtained possession of the fort, raising the cry of "No quarter!" But little opportunity was allowed for resistance. Our troops, black and white, threw down their arms, and sought to escape by running down the steep bluff near the fort, and secreting themselves behind trees and logs, in the bushes, and under the brush—some even jumping into the river, leaving only their heads above the water, as they crouched down under the bank.

Then followed a scene of cruelty and murder without a parallel in civilized warfare, which needed but the tomahawk and scalping-knife to exceed the worst atrocities ever committed by savages. The rebels commenced an indiscriminate slaughter, sparing neither age nor sex, white or black, soldier or civilian. The officers and men seemed to vie with each other in the devilish work; men, women, and even children, wherever found, were deliberately shot down, beaten, and hacked with sabers; some of the children not more than ten years old were forced to stand up and face their murders while being shot; the sick and the wounded were butchered without mercy, the rebels even entering the hospital building and dragging them out to be shot, or killing them as they lay there unable to offer the least resistance. All over the hillside the work of murder was going on; numbers of our men were collected together in lines or groups and deliberately shot; some were shot while in the river, while others on the bank were shot and their bodies kicked into the water, many of them still living but unable to make any exertions to save themselves from drowning. Some of the rebels stood on the top of the hill or a short distance down its side, and called to our soldiers to come up to them, and as they approached, shot them down in cold blood; if their guns or pistols miss fired, forcing them to stand there until they were again prepared to fire. All around were heard cries of "No quarter!" "No quarter!" "Kill the damned niggers; shoot them down!" All who asked for mercy were answered by the most cruel taunts and answers. Some were spared for a time, only to be murdered under circumstances of greater cruelty. No cruelty which the most fiendish malignity could devise was omitted by these murderers. One white soldier who was wounded in one leg so as to be unable to walk, was made to stand up and again shot. One negro who had been ordered by a rebel officer to hold his horse, was killed by him when he remounted; another, mere child, whom an officer had taken up behind him on his horse, was seen by Chalmers, who at once ordered the officer to put him down and shoot him, which was done. The huts and tents in which many of the wounded had sought shelter were set on fire, both that night and the next morning, while the wounded were still in them—those only escaping who were able to get themselves out, or who could prevail on others less injured than themselves to help them out; and even some of those thus seeking to escape the flames were met by these ruffins and brutally shot down, or had their brains beaten out. One man was deliberately fastened down to the floor of a tent, face upwards, by means of nails driven through his clothing and into the boards under him, so that he could not possibly escape, and then the tent set on fire; another was nailed to the side of a building outside of the fort, and then the building set on fire and burned. The charred remains of five or six bodies were afterwards found, all but one so much disfigured and consumed by the flames that they could not be identified, and the identification of that one is not absolutely certain, although there can hardly be a doubt that it was the body of Lieutenant Akerstrom, quartermaster of the 13th Tennessee cavalry, and a native Tennessean; several witnesses who saw the remains, and who were personally acquainted with him while living, have testified that it is their firm belief that it was his body that was thus treated. These deeds of murder and cruelty ceased when night came on, only to be renewed the next morning, when the demons carefully sought among the dead lying about in all directions for any of the wounded yet alive, and those they found were deliberately shot. Scores of the dead and wounded were found there the day after the massacre by the men from some of our gunboats who were permitted to go on shore and collect the wounded and bury the dead. The rebels themselves had made a pretense of burying a great many of their victims, but they had merely thrown them, without the least regard to care or decency, into the trenches and ditches about the fort, or the little hollows and ravines on the hill-side, covering them but partially with earth. Portions of heads and faces, hands and feet, were found protruding through the earth in every direction. The testimony also establishes the fact that the rebels buried some of the living with the dead, a few of whom succeeded afterwards in digging themselves out, or were dug out by others, one of whom your committee found in Mound City hospital, and there examined. And even when your committee visited the spot, two weeks afterwards, although parties of men had been sent on shore from time to time to bury the bodies unburied and rebury the others, and were even then engaged in the same work, we found the evidences of this murder and cruelty still most painfully apparent; we saw bodies still unburied (at some distance from the fort) of some sick men who had been met fleeing from the hospital and beaten down and brutally murdered, and their bodies left where they had fallen. We could still see the faces, hands, and feet of men, white and black, protruding out of the ground, whose graves had not been reached by those engaged in re-interring the victims of the massacre, and although a great deal of rain had fallen within the preceding two weeks, the ground, more especially on the side and at the foot of the bluff where most of the murders had been committed, was still discolored by the blood of our brave but unfortunate men, and the logs and trees showed but too plainly the evidences of the atrocities perpetrated there.

Many other instances of equally atrocious cruelty might be enumerated, but your committee feel compelled to refrain from giving here more of the heart sickening details, and refer to the statements contained in the voluminous testimony herewith submitted. Those statements were obtained by them from eyewitnesses and sufferers; many of them, as they were examined by your committee, were lying upon beds of pain and suffering, some so feeble that their lips could with difficulty frame the words by which they endeavored to convey some idea of the cruelties which had been inflicted on them, and which they had seen inflicted on others.

How many of our troops thus fell victim to the malignity and barbarity of Forrest and his followers cannot yet be definitely ascertained. Two officers belonging to the garrison were absent at the time of the capture and massacre. Of the remaining officers but two are known to be living, and they are wounded and now in the hospital at Mound City. One of these Captain Potter, may even now be dead, as the surgeons, when your committee were there, expressed no hope of his recovery. Of the men, from 300 to 400 are known to have been killed at Fort Pillow, of whom, at least, 300 were murdered in cold blood after the post was in possession of the rebels, and our men had thrown down their arms and ceased to offer resistance. Of the survivors, except the wounded in the hospital at Mound City, and the few who succeeded in making their escape unhurt, nothing definite is known; and it is to be feared that many have been murdered after being taken away from the fort. In reference to the fate of Major Bradford, who was in command of the fort when it was captured, and who had up to that time received no injury, there seems to be no doubt. The general understanding everywhere seemed to be that he had been brutally murdered the day after he was taken prisoner.

There is some discrepancy in the testimony, but your committee do not see how the one who professed to have been an eye-witness of his death could have been mistaken. There may be some uncertainty in regard to his fate.

When your committee arrived at Memphis, Tennessee, they found and examined a man (Mr. McLagan) who had been conscripted by some of Forrest's forces, but who, with other conscripts, had succeeded in making his escape. He testifies that while two companies of rebel troops, with Major Bradford and many other prisoners, were on their march from Brownsville to Jackson, Tennessee, Major Bradford was taken by five rebels—one an officer—led about fifty yards from the line of march and deliberately murdered in view of all there assembled. He fell—killed instantly by three musket balls, even while asking that his life might be spared, as he had fought them manfully, and was deserving of a better fate. The motive for the murder of Major Bradford seems to have been the simple fact that, although a native of the south, he remained loyal to his government. The testimony herewith submitted contains many statements made by the rebels that they did not intend to treat "home-made Yankees." as they termed loyal southerners, any better than ne-gro troops.

There is one circumstance connected with the events herein narrated which your committee cannot permit to pass unnoticed. The testimony herewith submitted disclosed this most astounding and shameful fate: On the morning of the day succeeding the capture of Fort Pillow, the gunboat *Silver Cloud,* (No. 28,) the transport *Platte Valley,* and the gunboat *New Era,* (No. 7,) landed at Fort Pillow under flag of truce, for the purpose of receiving the few wounded there and burying the dead. While they were lying there, the rebel General Chalmers and other rebel officers came down to the landing, and some of them went on the boats. Notwithstanding the evidences of rebel atrocity and barbarity with which the ground was covered, there were some of our army officers onboard the *Platte Valley* as lost to every feeling of decency, honor, and self-respect, as to make themselves disgracefully conspicuous in bestowing civilities and attention upon the rebel officers, even while they were boasting of the murders they had there committed. Your committee were unable to ascertain the names of the officers who have thus inflicted so foul a stain upon the honor or our army. They are assured, however, by the military authorities that every effort will be made to ascertain their names and bring them to the punishment they so richly merit. In relation to the re-enforcement or evacuation of Fort Pillow, it would appear from the testimony that the troops there statoned were withdrawn on the 25th of January last, in order to accompany the Meridian expedition under General Sherman. General Hurlbut testifies that he never received any instructions to permanently vacate the post, and deeming it important to occupy it, so that the rebels should not interrupt the navigation of the Mississippi by planting artillery there, he sent some troops there about the middle of February, increasing their number afterwards until the garrison mounted to nearly 600 men. He also states that as soon as he learned that the place was attacked, he immediately took measures to send up re-enforcements from Memphis, and they were actually embarking when he received information of the capture of the fort.

Your committee cannot close this report without expressing their obligations to the officers of the army and navy, with whom they were brought in contact, for the assistance they rendered. It is true your committee were furnished by the Secretary of War with the fullest authority to call upon any one in the army for such services as they might require, to enable them to make the investigation devolved upon them by Congress, but they found that no such authority was needed. The army and navy officers at every point they visited evinced a desire to aid the committee in every way in their power, and all expressed the highest satisfaction that Congress had so promptly taken steps to ascertain the facts connected with this fearful and bloody transaction, and the hope that the investigation would lead to prompt and decisive measures on the part of the government. Your committee would mention more particularly the names of General Mason Brayman, military commander at Cairo; Captain J. H. Odlin, his chief of staff; Captain Alexander M. Pennock, United State navy, fleet captain of Mississippi squadron; Captain James W. Shirk, United States navy, commanding 7th district Mississippi squadron; Surgeon Horace Wardner, in charge of Mound City general hospital; Captain Thomas M. Farrell, United States navy, in command of gunboat *Hastings,* furnished by (Captain Pennock to convey the committee to Fort Pillow and Memphis;) Captain Thomas Pattison, Naval commandant at Memphis, General C. C. Washburne, and the officers of their commands, as among, those to whom they are indebted for assistance and attention.

All of which is respectfully submitted.

B. W. Wade

D. W. Gooch

Adopted by the committee as their report.

B. F. Wade, Chairman.

Memphis Daily Appeal (Atlanta, Ga.) 2 May 1864

Movements of Gen. Forrest
Details of the Capture of Fort Pillow

Jackson, Tenn., April 18, 1864

Editors Appeal: The invincible and unconquered Forrest never wearies in his accustomed vocation. Each victory, although great, seems to be eclipsed by another still greater. The capture of Fort Pillow is one of the most brilliant achievements of the war. It has been regarded as Gibraltar. Our own people spent much money and labor in fortifying it. Since occupied by the Yankees they have added much to its strength. Nature has made it almost impregnable. But General Forrest, strong as it was known to be, conceived, the idea of storming and taking it.

For this purpose he left Jackson on the 19th [sic] of April with 1,200 picked men, composed principally of Gen. Chalmer's division. He went across the country like a flying cloud. He reached Fort Pillow the next morning, having traveled seventy two miles in twenty-four hours. He found the enemy's pickets posted upon the outer works and rushed them, capturing five out of seven. He then reached the second fortifica-

tion erected by the Confederates while Fort Pillow was held by them.
Here the enemy made a stubborn resistance for a few minutes, but our
troops rushed upon them with the velocity of the hurricane and drove
them rapidly into the main fortification from which they poured into
our ranks a terrible fire of ball and shell and grape and canister. In
order to protect his men, General Forrest ordered them to make a rapid
advance, about half way to the fort, where they would be protected by
the brow of the hill. From this place he sent a flag of truce to the enemy,
demanding an immediate and unconditional surrender. The enemy
asked for an hour's consideration. The object of the delay was evidently
to bring in reinforcements, and General Forrest refused the request,
demanding an immediate reply. In about seven minutes the enemy announced their determination not to surrender, and were accordingly
defiant and insolent in their demeanor. They ridiculed the idea of taking
the fort, and intimated that the last man would die before surrendering.
General Forrest told them that in order to prevent the effusion of blood
he had demanded the surrender, but now the consequences were upon
their heads.

He immediately commenced arranging his men for the assault. The
fort has only two sides, the other two being protected by the Mississippi
River and Coldwater. Between the river and the fort there is a space of
about eight feet left for the purpose of passing out down the river.
Coldwater is a narrow stream, and not, therefore, difficult to swim across.
In order to prevent any escape across the Coldwater, or through the
passage between the fort and the river, General Forrest stationed a part
of his command to guard these points. Everything being ready, he gave
the sign to sound the charge. The bugle was music to the eager Confederates. The first bugle caused a shout to burst from every throat, and
the impetuous braves went to the fort screaming like so many demons.
The enemy poured a murderous fire into our ranks, and several brave
spirits fell upon the wayside.

The walls of the fort are about eight feet thick and were of no advantage to the enemy after (we) reached it, as they could not fire without
getting upon top of the works, an experiment they did not attempt.
When our troops reached the fort, they found, what General Forrest
knew before, a ditch about seven feet deep; each man tumbled pell-mell
into this yawning chasm, and by assisting each other they were soon
found scaling the inner walls. In an instant a crop of armed men sprung
from the walls of the fort. They jumped down the inner walls screaming
and yelling like unearthly monsters.

Then the work of slaughter and death commenced. The sight of Negro troops stirred the bosoms of our soldiers with courageous madness.
The moment our men were seen upon the wall, the foe, which a few
minutes ago was so defiant and insolent, turned to cowards. Still they
would not surrender. Those that were hid or protected still kept firing
upon and killing our brave boys; but our troops still, rushed upon them,

all the time fighting and killing. The sight was terrific—the slaughter sickening. Wearied with the slow process of shooting with guns, our troops commenced with their repeaters, and every fire brought down a foe, and so close was the fight, that the dead would frequently fall upon the soldier that killed. Still the enemy would not or knew not how to surrender the Federal flag, that hated emblem of tyranny was still proudly waving over the scene. Seeing that nothing could be gained by further fight, the enemy rushed to the Coldwater for the purpose of swimming across; but the troops stationed here by General Forrest opened upon them, and hundreds were killed in the water endeavoring to escape. Others rushed to the passage between the fort and the river for the purpose of passing down the river towards Memphis. But the troops stationed here by General Forrest to guard this very contingency, opened fire upon them, and the enemy then rushed upon a coal barge and endeavored to push it off; but a concentrated fire from our whole column, soon put an end to this experiment. Several hundred were shot in this boat and in Coldwater, while endeavoring to escape. The number in the water was so great, that they resembled a drove of hogs swimming across the stream. But not a man escaped in this way. The head above the water was a beautiful mark for the trusty rifle of our unerring marksmen. The Mississippi River was crimsoned with red blood of the flying foe. Our soldiers grew sick and weary in the work of slaughter, and were glad when the work was done.

General Forrest begged them to surrender, but he was told with an air of insulting defiance that he could not take the place, and that they asked for no quarter. Not the first sign of surrender was ever given. General Forrest expected a surrender after entering the fort, and anxiously looked for it, as he witnessed the carnage; but no token was given.

In order to divert the attention of the enemy General Forrest ordered a simultaneous feint upon Memphis, Columbus and Paducah. This strategic movement was eminently successful, accomplished the very object he desired. But the feint upon Paducah was more of a victory. General Buford in obedience to orders from General Forrest attacked Paducah. He sent in a flag of truce, demanding a surrender of the town or an immediate removal of the women and children. The enemy would not make the surrender, but sent out the women, children and non-combatants. General Buford then rushed upon the town killing and capturing several of the enemy. They poured upon him a terrible fire from the forts and gunboats, but he did not lose a man. He captured several hundred horses, wagons, harness, etc., and after loading the wagons with such articles as he needed, he entered and conscribed all the non-combatants liable to military duty. Several of the enemy's pickets were killed at Columbus and the enemy expected a general assault. The same thing was expected at Memphis. But the real design as before stated was to divert their attention from Fort Pillow.

Our loss at Fort Pillow will reach near one hundred killed and wounded. I regret to announce, that Col. W. B. Reed, of Tennessee, was mortally wounded. While gallantly leading his regiment and planting his standard in front of the enemy, he received three wounds, one of which is feared will prove mortal. He is a gallant officer, and has won upon all hearts during his short connection with his command. He is known for his piety and integrity, and is beloved by all. He won imperishable renown in the late fight.

Memphis

Notes

Abbreviations

CR   Congressional Report of Fort Pillow Massacre
CSA   Confederate States of America
OR   Offical Records of Civil War
RG,NA   Muster Rolls Record Group, National Archives
USCT   U.S. Colored Troops
USCLA   U.S. Colored Light Artillery
USCHA   U.S. Colored Heavy Artillery

Introduction

1. Francis Trevelyan Miller, *The Photographic History of the Civil War*, Vol. 10 (New York: The Reviews of Reviews Co., 1911), 142–44.

2. "The butcher's bill" for the entire four years of conflict came to 1,094,453 casualties. Among 2,000,000 Federal servicemen, 640,000 were counted as casualies. In comparison the Confederates reported 750,000 men in arms with 450,000 casualties. The Federals lost approximately 110,000 killed in battle and the Confederates 94,000. Death from disease and assorted causes are estimated at 255,000 for the Federals and 162,000 for the Confederates. Among the wounded, the North reported 275,000 and the South 194,000. These figures were accumulated in more than 10,000 military actions that included 76 full scale battles, 310 engagements, 6,337 skirmishes, numerous seiges, raids, and expeditions (Shelby Foote, ed., *Red River to Appomatox* [New York: Simon and Schuster, 1960], 1040).

3. Robert Selph Henry, *Nathan Bedford Forrest, First with the Most* (New York: Mallard Press, 1991), 14.

4. Paul M. Angle, and Earl Schneck Meir, *The Tragic Years*, Vol. II (New York: Simon and Schuster, 1960), 754.

5. Albert Castel reports the garrison was composed of 557: 326 survived, 226 taken prisoner, 100 wounded, and 231 died (Albert Castel, "Fort Pillow: Victory or Massacre," *American History Illustrated* [April 1974], 47).

Dr. Wyeth reports the strength of the garrison at 557: with 336 survivors, of whom 226 were prisoners and 130 wounded, 206 unwounded and 221 killed (John A. Wyeth, *The Life of General Nathan Bedford Forrest* [1899; reprinted as *That Devil Forrest: The Life of General Nathan Bedford Forrest*, New York: Harper and Brothers, 1959], 332–33; shortened references herein refer to the 1899 publication as *Life of Forrest* and the 1959 reprint as *Devil Forrest*).

Cimprich and Mainfort, Jr. assembled the most thorough and studied analysis of Federal strength and casualties. They indicate the garrison was composed of between 585 and 605 mixed troops, total deaths ranged between 47 and 49 percent with black units suffering 64 percent fatalities (John Cimprich and Robert C. Mainfort Jr., "The Fort Pillow Massacre: A Statistical Note," *Journal of American History* [December 1989], 836 and 837).

Henry estimated the garrison's strength at 557 with 231 killed. He concludes 226 were taken prisoner and 100 wounded (Henry, *First with the Most*, 258 and 259).

Jordan claims the garrison consisted of 580, 182 of whom were killed and 398 survived: 226 taken prisoner, 130 wounded, and 42 other (John L. Jordan, "Was There a Massacre at Fort Pillow?" *Tennessee Historical Quarterly* [June 1947], 111–14).

General Jordan and Pryor estimated the garrison did not exceed 580 although they account for only 557 and that 55 percent of the garrison survived, and 40 percent were unhurt. This figure computes to 261 killed, 87 wounded, and 232 survivors (General Thomas Jordan and J. P. Pryor, *The Campaign of Lieut.–Gen. N. B. Forrest, and of Forrest's Cavalry* [Ohio: Morningside Bookshop, 1988], 428 and 444).

Records furnished by Lieutenant Colonel Harris in Memphis (OR, Vol. 32, Series I, Part I, p. 556) indicated the garrison had on record several weeks before the engagement a complement of 557 officers and men. These figures are generally conceded as stale, not reflective of current returns, and unreliable as to men serving at the fort with the 13th Tennessee Cavalry who had enlisted but had not been mustered into service.

The author has chosen the figure of 578 which includes several on detached duty with the garrison and excludes five known to have been in Memphis at the time of the attack and nine civilians known to have participated in the fort's defense, one of whom was killed. At the time of the attack at least twenty servicemen were convalesants at the fort's hospital.

6. Henry, *First with the Most*, 259.

7. Bruce Catton, *Army of the Potomac; Mr. Lincoln's Army* (New York: Doubleday and Company, Inc., 1951, 1962), 189.

8. Three reports furnished by General Forrest dated 15 April (OR, Vol. 32, Series I, Part I, 609, 610, 612) and one dated 26 April (OR, Vol. 32, Series I, Part I, 616) give his losses at twenty killed and sixty wounded. Cimprich and Mainfort, Jr., *Fort Pillow Revisited*, page 295, footnote 8, claim the Confederate Collection of the Tennessee State Library and Archives, Nashville, Tennessee, reports Forrest's losses at 13 dead and 83 wounded. General Chalmers reported casualties of 14 killed and 86 wounded (OR, Vol. 32, Series I, Part I, 622).

9. See chap. 2, "Attack on Fort Pillow." There were approximately 284 blacks and 294 white officers and men.

10. Gordan and Pryor, *Campaigns of Forrest*, 704.

11. Wyeth, *Devil Forrest*, 337.

12. Foote, *Red River to Appomatox*, 111.

13. OR, Vol. 32, Series I, Part I, 571; OR Vol. 26, Series I, 231–32.

Chapter 1. The Devil Forrest

1. Henry, *First with the Most*, 23.

2. Ibid., 439.

3. Carl Sandburg quipped: "As a slave trader he had the faint enigmatic odor of something or other that traditionally excluded slave-traders from exclu-

sive social circles of the South" (Carl Sandburg, *Abraham Lincoln, The War Years,* Vol. III [New York: Harcourt Brace and World, Inc., 1939], 37).

4. Henry, *First with the Most,* 15.

5. Ibid., 439. Testimony given before *Joint Select Committee to Inquire into the Condition of Affairs in the Late Insurrectionary States* (Klu Klux Klan Investigation of 1872), 42d Congress, 2d Session, Senate Report No. 41, Vol. 13, 24.

6. Wyeth, *Devil Forrest,* 6.

7. Henry, *First with the Most,* 23.

8. Ibid., 13.

9. Wyeth, *Devil Forrest,* xx.

10. Ibid., 558.

11. Ibid., xx; Henry, *First with the Most,* 15; Lafcadio Hearn, *Occidental Gleanings* ed. Albert Mordell (New York: Dodd, Mead and Co., 1929), 145; Wyeth, *Devil Forrest,* xxv.

12. Hearn, *Occidental Gleanings,* 145–48.

13. Glenn Tucker, "Nathan B. Forrest," *Untutored Genius of the War* (Jamestown, Va.: Eastern Acorn Press, 1988), 17.

14. Wyeth, *Devil Forrest,* 15 and 16.

15. Henry, *First With the Most,* 162–63.

16. Gary W. Gallagher, ed., *Fighting for the Confederacy: The Personal Recollections of General Edward Porter Alexander* (Chapel Hill and London: The University of North Carolina Press, 1989), 295.

17. Wyeth, *Life of Forrest,* 264–66; Henry, *First with the Most,* 198–99.

18. Wyeth, *Devil Forrest,* 279.

19. Ibid., 571.

20. Wyeth, *Life of Forrest,* 629–30.

21. Ibid., 91–92.

22. Henry, *First with the Most,* 19.

23. Ibid., 13 and 471.

24. Ibid., 16; Wyeth, *Devil Forrest,* 342; OR, Vol. 39, Series I, Part I, 121.

25. William Tecumseh Sherman, *Memoirs of General W. T. Sherman* (New York: The Library of America, 1990), 363.

26. Ulysses S. Grant, *Personal Memoirs and Selected Letters,* Vol. II (New York: The Library of America, 1990), 346.

27. Wyeth, *Devil Forrest,* 560.

28. Wyeth, *Life of Forrest,* 622.

Chapter 2. Attack on Fort Pillow

1. "The object of the Meridian expedition was to strike the roads inland (General William Sooy Smith, leaving from Memphis, was to link up with Sherman at Meridian, Mississippi, with the latter starting from Vicksburg) so as to paralyze the rebel forces that we could take from the defenses of the Mississippi River the equivalent of a corps of 20,000 men, to be used in the next Georgia Campaign; and this was actually done. At the same time, I wanted to destroy General Forrest, who, with an irregular force of cavalry, was constantly threatening Memphis and the river above, as well as our routes of supply in Middle Tennessee. In this we failed utterly, because General W. Sooy Smith did not fulfill his orders." (Sherman, *Memoirs,* 422–23).

2. Sherman, *Memoirs,* 429, 463, 486.

3. Sherman, *Memoirs*, 464. By 10 April 1865 out of the Military Divisions of the Mississippi, he organized elements of three armies, that by 1 May 1864, contained 98,797 men and 254 guns (Ibid., 472, 473, 487).

4. OR, Vol. 32, Series I, Part II, 326.

5. Ibid., 593, 594; Wyeth, *Devil Forrest*, 586, 300; Henry, *First with the Most*, 235–36.

6. Henry, *First with the Most*, 237.

7. Ibid., 238.

8. OR, Vol. 32, Series I, Pt. III, 118.

9. Ibid., 117.

10. Ibid., 119.

11. OR, Vol. 32, Series I, Part I, 585, 623.

12. Henry, *First with the Most*, 239.

13. OR, Vol. 32, Series I, Part I, 540.

14. Ibid., 545.

15. Wyeth, *Devil Forrest*, 303; Henry, *First with the Most*, 239.

16. OR, Vol. 32, Series I, Part I, 542–45.

17. Ibid., 541.

18. Ibid., 509.

19. Ibid., 548.

20. Ibid., 547.

21. Ibid., 547.

22. Ibid., 511.

23. Ibid., 505.

24. Ibid., 548.

25. Ibid., 548.

26. Ibid., 608.

27. Ibid., 552.

28. Ibid., 549.

29. Ronald K. Huch, "The Fort Pillow Massacre: The Aftermath of Paducah," *Journal of the Illinois State Historical Society* 66 (Spring 1966), 68.

30. Two fifths or 274 blacks from the First Kentucky Heavy Artillery comprised a part of Hick's aggregate of 665 men (OR, Vol. 32, Series I, Part I, 548).

31. Henry, *First with the Most*, 243.

32. OR, Vol. 32, Series I, Part I, 609.

33. OR, Vol. 32, Series I, Part III, 759.

34. OR, Vol. 32, Series I, Part I, 553.

35. Ibid.

36. Ibid., 550.

37. OR, Vol. 32, Series I, Part II, 159–60.

38. Born in 1806, General Pillow was a criminal lawyer, who held the rank of brigadier general during the Mexican War and was promoted to major general by his law partner, President James K. Polk. As commander of Fort Donnelson, he is remembered for relinquishing the command at a time when the garrison was surrounded by Grant's troops and further resistance would have been futile. He then made his escape before the Confederates surrendered to General Grant.

39. Sherman, *Memoirs*, 277.

40. Wyeth, *Life of Forrest*, 334.

41. General Chalmers, OR, Vol. 32, Series I, Part I, 621.

42. Ibid., 595; Charles Anderson, "Confederate Veteran," *The True Story of Fort Pillow*, Vol. 3 (November 1895), 322.

43. OR, Vol. 32, Series I, Part I, 614.

44. Ibid., 556.

45. Ibid., 568.

46. John L. Jordan, "Was There a Massacre at Fort Pillow?" 105–6.

47. Cimprich and Mainfort, Jr., *Fort Pillow Revisited*, 294, n.5.

48. OR, Vol. 32, Series I, Part I, 556.

49. Sherman, *Memoirs*, 237.

50. OR, Vol. 32, Series I, Part III, 327.

51. OR, Vol. 32, Series I, Part I, 556.

52. Ibid., 557.

53. CR, 65.

54. OR, Vol. 32, Series I, Part I, 621.

55. Ibid., 559.

56. Ibid., 612.

57. Logs of United States Naval Ships, RG 24, NA.

58. OR, Vol. 32, Series I, Part I, 614.

59. General Chalmers was in error. Only the *New Era* was on station, and the fort possessed six pieces of artillery.

60. OR, Vol. 32, Series I, Part I, 621.

61. Ibid., 595–96.

62. Ibid., 596.

63. Ibid., 560.

64. Ibid., 596.

65. Ibid., 560.

66. Ibid., 561.

67. Ibid., 570.

68. Ibid., 561.

69. Cimprich and Mainfort, Jr., *Fort Pillow Revisited*, 299.

70. Ibid., 302.

71. Sandburg, *Lincoln: War Years*, 38.

72. OR, Vol. 32, Series I, Part I, 520.

73. Ibid., 521.

74. Ibid., 522.

75. Ibid., 530.

76. Ibid., 533.

77. Ibid., 522.

78. Ibid., 522. In the Cimprich and Mainfort, Jr. article, *Fort Pillow Revisited*, 302–5, a report from Lieutenant Colonel Thomas J. Jackson is quoted in which he fictionalizes the heroism of Private Eli Cothel. Colonel Jackson describes Cothel, despite his three wounds, as having miraculously secreted the trampled Union flag inside his shirt and later, while at the hospital, presenting it to Mrs. Booth. The flag was actually taken by Forrest and forwarded to Richmond for display. Cothel was shot only twice (Congressional Report, 55); his rank was that of a Corporal and not a private; and in his affidavit (OR, Vol. 32, Series I, Part I, 522) he conspicuously makes no reference to the incident. Nor does the event find reference in any of the official records or correspondence.

79. OR, Vol. 32, Series I, Part I, 523.

80. Ibid., 523.

81. Ibid., 527.

82. Ibid., 524.
83. Ibid., 526.
84. Ibid., 525.
85. Ibid., 528–29.
86. Ibid., 531.
87. Ibid., 532.
88. Ibid., 532.
89. Ibid., 534–36.
90. Ibid., 537.
91. Ibid., 539.
92. Some members of both the black and white units had not been mustered into service at the time of the attack.
93. OR, Vol. 32, Series I, Part I, 559–63.
94. CR, 37–42.
95. Ibid., 34, 43.
96. Ibid., 42.
97. Ibid., 83.
98. Ibid., 82.
99. OR, Vol. 32, Series I, Part I, 565.
100. Dr. Charles Fitch, "Dr. Fitch's Report on the Fort Pillow Massacre," *Tennessee Historical Quarterly* 44 (Spring 1985), 31.
101. OR, Vol. 32, Series I, Part I, 564.
102. Jordan, *Campaigns of Forrest*, 455; Wyeth, *Devil Forrest*, 587–88.
103. OR, Vol. 32, Series I, Part I, 557; CR, 101–3.
104. OR, Vol. 32, Series I, Part I, 567.
105. Special Order No. 150, 17 April 1864 (OR, Vol. 32, Part III, 397). Grant actually relieved General Hurlbut on 15 April 1864 (OR, Vol. 32, Part III, 366).
106. OR, Vol. 32, Series I, Part I, 587.
107. Ibid., 588.
108. Ibid., 589.
109. Ibid., 592–93.
110. Ibid., 599–600.
111. Ibid., 604.
112. Ibid., 601.
113. Ibid., 610.
114. Ibid., 612.
115. Ibid., 617.
116. Ibid., 608–9.
117. Ibid., 604, 605.
118. Ibid., 618.
119. Ibid., 623.

Chapter 3. Anxiety in the Public Mind

1. OR, Vol. 26, Series I, 221.
2. Ibid., 222.
3. *New York Times,* 20 April 1964.
4. Charles Anderson, "The True Story of Fort Pillow," *Confederate Veteran* (November 1895), 322–25.
5. *New York Times,* 16 April 1864.

6. *New York Times,* 20 April 1864.

7. *The Evening Post,* 21 April 1864.

8. CR, 7.

9. Anderson, *True Story,* 325.

10. *New York Times,* 20 April 1864.

11. *New York Times,* 24 April 1864.

12. *Evening Post,* 15 April 1865.

13. *New York Times,* 16 April 1864.

14. *Evening Post,* 22 April 1864.

15. OR, Vol. 32, Series I, Part I, 563.

16. Ibid., 555.

17. OR, Vol. 32, Series I, Part III, 364.

18. Fatigue duties included unloading vessels, filling sandbags, burial details, and building entrenchments. War Department Special Order No. 13 of April 1863 assigned black units to the additional duties of securing abandoned cotton and attending to its shipment to Memphis (Benjamin Quarles, *The Negro in the Civil War* [New York: Russell & Russell, 1987], 205).

19. James McPherson, *The Negroes Civil War* (New York: Pantheon Books, 1965), 221.

20. *Evening Post,* 18 April 1864.

21. John J. Nicolay and John Hay, Vol. X, *The Sponsors Edition of the Complete Works of Abraham Lincoln* (Lincoln Memorial University, 1897), 78–80.

22. Angle and Miers, *Tragic Years,* Vol. II, 760.

23. Dudley Taylor Cornish, *The Sable Arm: Black Troops in the Union Army, 1861–1865* (Lawrence: University Press of Kansas, 1987), 176; Sandburg, Vol. 3, *Lincoln War Years,* 43.

24. Ibid.

Chapter 4. An Unavoidable Loss

1. General Forrest estimated his forces under General Chalmers at fifteen hundred. (OR, Vol. 32, Series I, Part I, 609). see also: Castel, *Fort Pillow Massacre,* 39; Henry, *First with the Most,* 250. Wyeth stated three hundred Confederates were assigned as sharpshooters, and Colonels McCulloch and Bell were each given eight hundred men. (Wyeth, *Storming of Fort Pillow,* 596). Achilles Clark estimated an additional detachment of one fourth of the original forces were assigned to holding the horses (Dan E. Pomeroy, ed., "Achilles Clark: A Letter of Account," *Civil War Times Illustrated* 24 [June 1985], 24).

2. OR, Vol 32, Series I, Part I, 596.

3. Wyeth, "The Storming of Fort Pillow," *Harpers New Monthly Magazine* 99, no. 592 (1869), 603.

4. OR, Vol. 32, Series I, Part I, 596.

5. Ibid., 561.

6. Ibid., 527, 561, 570.

7. Wyeth, *Devil Forrest,* 320.

8. Jordan and Pryor, *Campaigns of Forrest,* 433.

9. See Henry, *First with the Most,* 253.

10. Castel, *Fort Pillow Massacre,* 41–42.

11. Henry, *First with the Most,* 252.

12. Logs of U.S. Naval Ships, RG 24, NA, quoted in Cimprich and Mainfort, Jr., *Fort Pillow Revisited,* 294–95.

13. Jordan and Pryor, *Campaigns of Forrest*, 435.

14. Wyeth, *Devil Forrest*, 319.

15. George Bodnia, ed., "Fort Pillow Massacre: Observations of a Minnesotan," *Minnesota Historical Society* (Spring 1973), 186–90.

16. Wyeth, *Devil Forrest*, 321.

17. Henry, *First with the Most*, 254.

18. CR, 86; OR, Vol. 26, Series I, 221.

19. OR, Vol. 26, Series I, 219.

20. OR, Vol. 32, Series I, Part III, 520.

21. CR, 86.

22. Jordan and Pryor, *Campaigns of Forrest*, 438.

23. CR, 97.

24. OR, Vol. 32, Series I, Part I, 345–47.

25. Ibid., 347.

26. Wyeth, *Life of Forrest*, 339; Jordan and Pryor, *Campaigns of Forrest*, 425.

27. OR, Vol. 32, Series I, Part I, 346.

28. Ibid., 504.

29. OR, Vol. 32, Series I, Part III, 382.

30. Ibid., 376.

31. OR, Vol. 32, Series I, Part I, 516.

32. CR, 65.

33. OR, Vol. 32, Series I, Part III, 367.

34. Special Field Orders No. 6 dated 2 February from the Sixteenth Army Corps at Vicksburg, directed Major Bradford to immediately occupy Fort Pillow with his entire command. General Smith's correspondence of the previous day was written from Memphis. (OR, Vol. 32, Series I, Part III, 317, 318).

35. CR, 97.

36. OR, Vol. 32, Series I, Part III, 177.

37. Ibid., 336; OR, Vol. 32, Series I, Part I, 555. There is no explanation in the record why General Hurlbut learned of the engagement two hours after Lieutenant Commander Pattison, when they were both stationed at Memphis.

38. OR, Vol. 32, Series I, Part III, 366, 367.

39. Ibid., 381.

Chapter 5. An Indiscriminate Slaughter

1. Jordan and Pryor, *Campaigns of Forrest*, 442.

2. Wyeth, *Devil Forrest*, 341.

3. CR, 1–2.

4. CR, 3.

5. Wyeth, *Storming Fort Pillow*, 595.

6. Jordan and Pryor, *Campaigns of Forrest*, 444.

7. CR, 43.

8. The phrase "indiscriminate slaughter" did not originate with the subcommittee's report. Extensive use of this or similar phraseology can be found in newspaper articles, witness affidavits, or official correspondence predating the Congressional Report.

9. Henry, *First with the Most*, 261.

10. Jordan and Pryor, *Campaings of Forrest*, 439.

11. Wyeth, *Devil Forrest*, 339.

12. Ibid., 327.

13. Anderson, *The True Story*, 324; Castel, *Fort Pillow Massacre*, 324.

14. Wyeth, *Life of Forrest*, 355.

15. CR, 86.

16. Jordan and Pryor, *Campaigns of Forrest*, 437.

17. Anderson, *The True Story*, 324.

18. OR, Vol. 32, Series I, Part I, 616.

19. Castel, *Fort Pillow Massacre*, 43.

20. OR, Vol. 32, Series I, Part I, 539.

21. Ibid., 567.

22. Ibid., 564.

23. Ibid., 615.

24. ibid., 612.

25. "On the morning of the fight there was so much hurry and confusion that our flag was not raised for a time; we had been firing away an hour before I happened to notice that our flag was not up. I ordered it to be raised immediately, and our troops set up vociferous cheers, especially the colored troops, who entered into the fight with great energy and spirit" (CR, 41).

26. Wyeth, *Devil Forrest*, 329.

27. OR, Vol. 32, Series I, Part I, 615; Anderson, *The True Story*, 323, Forrest's last expression was to "fight everything 'blue' between wind and water until yonder flag comes down."

28. Henry, *First with the Most*, 264–65.

29. Wyeth, *Devil Forrest*, 323; Jordan & Pryor, *Campaigns of Forrest*, 439.

30. Wyeth, *Devil Forrest*, 592–95.

31. Wyeth, *Life of Forrest*, 350; Wyeth, *Storming Fort Pillow*, 603.

32. Charles Fitch, "Letter to Gen. Chalmers," 13 May 1979, *Southern Historical Society Papers* 7 (13 May 1979), 440–41.

33. Wyeth, *Life of Forrest*, 367.

34. CR, 84–86; OR, Vol. 32, Series I, Part I, 524, 528.

35. Mainfort, Jr., *Archaeological Investigation*, 37.

36. See Benjamin Quarles, *The Negro in the Civil War*, 58–61.

37. Cornish, *Sable Arm*, 228.

38. Joseph T. Glatthaar, *Forged in Battle: The Civil War Alliance of Black Soldiers and White Officers* (London: The Free Press, 1990), 53; Quarles, *Negro Civil War*, 209.

39. Glatthaar, *Forged in Battle*, 39.

40. McPherson, *Negro's Civil War*, 216.

41. George Williams, *A History of Negro Troops in the War of the Rebellion* (New York: Negro University Press, 1969), xiv.

42. Castel, *Fort Pillow Massacre*, 44.

43. "[T]hey made a wild, crazy scattering fight. They acted like a crowd of drunken men. They would, at one moment, yield and throw down their guns, and then would rush again to arms, seize their guns and renew the fire. If one squad was left as prisoners ... it was soon discovered that they could not be trusted as having surrendered, for taking the first opportunity they would break loose again and engage in the contest. Some of our men were killed by negroes who had once surrendered" (Henry, *First with the Most*, 256).

44. OR, Vol. 32, Series I, Part I, 528.

45. CR, 82.

46. Ibid., 85.

47. Ibid., 100.

48. Jordan and Pryor, *Campaigns of Forrest,* 434.

49. Wyeth, *Devil Forrest,* 322.

50. CR, 43.

51. Ibid., 15, 16, 18, 21, 22, 30, 43, 45, 47, 51, 89, 96.

52. Ibid., 26, 33, 37, 43.

53. Ibid., 20, 22, 47, 58, 85.

54. Ibid., 90.

55. Ibid., 51.

56. Ibid., 53.

57. Ibid., 13, 43, 88, 94.

58. Ibid., 31, 39, 76, 83, 91.

59. Ibid., 27, 30, 52, 61, 90, 94. Eli A. Bangs, Master's Mate for the *New Era,* stated:

> Question: Did you see any peculiar marks of barbarity, as inflicted upon the dead?
>
> Answer. I saw none that I noticed, except in the case of one black man that I took up off a tent floor. He lay on his back, with his arms stretched out. Part of his arms were burned off, and his legs were burned nearly to a crisp. His stomach was bare. The clothes had either been torn off, or burned off. In order to take away the remains, I slipped some pieces of board under him, and when we took him up the boards of the tent camp up with him; and we then observed that nails had been driven through his clothes and his cartridge-box, so as to fasten him down to the floor. His face was not burned, but was very much distorted, as if he had died in great pain. Several others noticed the nails through his clothes which fastened him down.
>
> Question. Do you think there can be any doubt about his having been nailed to the boards?
>
> Answer. I think not, from the fact that the boards came up with the remains as we raised them up; and we then saw the nails sticking through his clothes, and into the boards.
>
> Question. Did you notice any other bodies that had been burned?
>
> Answer. Yes sir; I buried four that had been burned.

60. CR, 17, 18, 95.

61. Williams, *History of Negro Troops,* 265–66.

62. CR, 13, 14.

63. CR, 93.

64. OR, Vol. 32, Series I, Part I, 558.

65. CR, 100.

66. Pomeroy, Dan E., ed. "Letter of Account: Sergeant Clark Tells of the Fort Pillow Massacre," *Civil War Times Illustrated* 24 (June 1985), 24–25.

67. Cimprich and Mainfort, Jr., *Fort Pillow Revisited,* 300.

68. CR, 34.

69. OR, Vol. 32, Series I, Part III, 381.

70. Ibid., 381.

71. Ibid., 367.

72. Ibid., 369.

73. Foote, *Red River to Appomatox,* 112.

74. Henry, *First with the Most,* 268.

75. OR, Vol. 32, Series I, Part III, 464.

76. Sherman, *Memoirs,* 470.

77. OR, Vol. 39, Part III, 494.

78. Sherman, *Memoirs,* 470.

79. OR, Vol. 3, Series III, 148–64.

80. Ibid., 151.

81. OR, Vol. 32, Series I, Part III, 383–411.

82. Cornish, *Sable Arm*, 178.

83. Cornish, *Sable Arm*, 179.

84. Nicolay and Hay, *Abraham Lincoln*, Vol. X, 80.

85. OR, Vol. 32, Series I, Part III, 464.

86. Lois D. Bejach, "DeWitt Clinton Fort," *West Tennessee Historical Society Papers* 2 (1948), 19.

87. Cornish, *Sable Arm*, 158.

88. OR, Vol. 4, Series II, 954.

89. OR, Vol. 5, Series II, 807–8.

90. Ibid., 940, 941.

91. OR, Vol. 6, Series I, 77–78.

92. For a full discussion of both northern and southern attitudes, see Cornish, *The Sable Arm*, 157–78.

93. Sandburg, *War Years*, Vol. III, 37.

94. OR, Vol. 32, Series I, Part I, 600.

95. Ibid., 623.

96. Henry, *First with the Most*, 261.

97. Wyeth, *Life of Forrest*, 366.

98. Cimprich and Mainfort, Jr., *Fort Pillow Revisited*, 295.

99. Jordan and Pryor, *Campaigns of Forrest*, 422–23; General Sherman gave specific orders on 6 January 1864 to the commanding general for the Columbus, Kentucky and Jackson, Tennessee military district as to how the countryside in and about Fort Pillow was to be treated. "There is no need of haste, but punish the country well for permitting the guerrillas among them. Take freely the horses, mules, cattle, &c., of the hostile or indifferent inhabitants, and let them all understand that if from design or weakness they permit their country to be used by the public enemy they must bear the expense of the troops sent to expel them; also notify them that we will soon begin to banish all people who are deemed opposed to the re-establishment of civil order. I want your cavalry to feed high and have their horses in good order. This cold weather is hard on your men, and they should be allowed to use freely the houses and fuel of the country. The people must expect us to treat them as enemies, unless they assist us in our efforts to restore civil order. Jackson, Trenton and Brownsville deserve no mercy at our hands, but in counties where the people have acted properly a broad distinction should be made. I attach no importance to oaths or opinions, but the people must be construed friends or enemies according to their general behavior. I want to hear from you about the 12th or 13th instant" (OR, Vol. 32, Part II, Series I, 36).

100. OR, Vol. 32, Series I, Part III, 609, 612, 625, 664.

101. Cornish, *Sable Arm*, 175.

102. OR, Vol. 32, Series I, Part I, 609, 610, 615.

103. Brian Steele Wills, *A Battle from the Start: The Life of Nathan Bedford Forrest* (New York: Harper & Collins, 1992), 194.

104. Huch, *Aftermath of Paducah*, 68–69.

105. OR, Vol. 32, Series I, Part I, 615.

106. CR, 22, 40, 43.

107. Ibid., 15.

108. Ibid., 16.

109. Ibid., 21.

110. Ibid., 43, 46.

111. Ibid., 47.

112. Ibid., 45.

113. Ibid., 32.

114. Cimprich and Mainfort, Jr., *Dr. Fitch's Report,* 36.

115. CR, 18.

116. CR, 24, 26.

117. CR, 27, 34, 45, 46, 49.

118. CR, 51.

119. CR, 52.

120. OR, Vol. 32, Series I, Part I, 558.

121. CR, 85.

122. CR, 89.

123. CR, 102.

124. OR, Vol. 32, Series I, Part I, 513.

125. James R. Chalmers, "Nathan Bedford Forrest and His Campaigns," *Southern Historical Society Papers* 7 (August 1879), 448, 471.

126. Castel, *Victory or Massacre,* 7.

127. Henry, *First with the Most,* 261–62.

128. Jack Hurst, *Nathan Bedford Forrest* (New York: Alfred A. Knopf, 1993), 177.

129. Jordan and Pryor, *Campaigns of Forrest,* 431.

130. In December 1884, Sherman outside of Savannah told General Hardee, CSA, that should he be forced to assault the city or resort to some slower process, he would feel justified and would "make little effort to restrain (his) army." Sherman felt he was merely echoing the demands of General J. B. Hood, CSA, who two months previously threatened the Federal garrison at Rasaca, Georgia, that if the place is carried by assault, no prisoners will be taken. (Sherman, *Memoirs,* 687, 630).

131. Wills, *Battle from the Start,* 185.

Chapter 6. Tides of Wrath

1. OR, Vol. 32, Series I, Part I, 619.

2. Jordan and Pryor, *Campaigns of Forrest,* 704. This list conspicuously omits Major Bradford's name. Some historians claim this list contains prisoners who were actually captured elsewhere.

3. Mainfort, Jr., *Archaeological Investigation,* 88–89.

4. Roy P. Basler, "And for His Widow and His Orphans," *Quarterly Journal of the Library of Congress,* Vol. 27 (27 October 1970), 292.

5. Ibid., 292.

6. Ibid., 294.

7. Cimprich and Mainfort, Jr., *Dr. Fitch's Report,* 29.

8. McPherson, *Battle Cry of Freedom,* 791–92.

9. Williams, *History of the Negro Troops,* 318–19.

10. Grant, *Memoirs,* 1048.

11. OR, Vol. 7, Series II, 203–4.

12. Quoted in Glatthaar, *Forged in Battle,* 156. See OR, Vol. 34, Series I, Part I, 743–57.

13. Cornish, *Sable Arm,* 177.

14. McPherson, *Battle Cry of Freedom,* 793; OR, Vol. 7, Series I, 459–60.

15. Federal Surgeon William Gardner reported three separate occasions when Confederate soldiers stormed into the field hospital and the Emory and Henry College Hospital killing Negro troops and their officers. (OR, Vol. 39, Part I, Series I, pp. 554–55, 557).

16. Glatthaar, *Forged in Battle,* 157.

17. Bodnia, *Observation of a Minnesotan,* 190.

18. OR, Vol. 32, Series I, Part III, 364.

19. Glatthaar, *Forged in Battle,* 157–58.

20. Ibid., 200.

21. Cornish, *Sable Arm,* 177.

22. John F. Brobst, *Civil War Letters of a Wisconsin Volunteer* (Madison: University of Wisconsin Press, 1960), 56–57.

23. Robert Hale Strong, *Yankee Private's Civil War,* Ashley Halsey, ed. (Chicago: Henry Regney Company, 1961), 15–16.

24. McPherson, *Negro's Civil War,* 230–31.

25. Ibid., 222.

26. *Philadelphia Press,* 12 July 1864.

27. Henry, *First with the Most,* 283.

28. Ibid., 300; *Civil War Times,* 10.

29. Henry, *First with the Most,* 300.

30. Ibid., 303.

31. Bennett H. Young, *Confederate Wizards of the Saddle* (Dayton, Ohio: Morningside House, Inc., 1988), 6.

32. Wyeth, *Life of Forrest,* 476.

33. James R. Chalmers, "Nathan Bedford Forrest and His Campaigns," *Southern Historical Society Papers* 7, no. 10 (October 1979), 472.

34. A copy of the indictment may be obtained from Archivist, National Archives–Southeast Region, 1557 St. Joseph Avenue, East Point, Georgia 30844 for a nominal fee.

35. Henry, *First with the Most,* 448.

36. McPherson, *Negro's Civil War,* 223.

37. Cornish, *Sable Arm,* 289.

38. *Rhode Island Soldiers & Sailors Historical Society,* No. 113, Series 3, Providence, 1885, 11–48.

39. CR, 30.

Select Bibliography

Anderson, Charles. "The True Story of Fort Pillow." *Confederate Veteran* 3 (November 1895), 322–26.

Angle, Paul M., and Earl Schneck Miers. *The Tragic Years, 1860–1865.* Vol. 3. New York: Simon and Schuster Company, 1960.

Basler, Roy P. "And for His Widow and His Orphan." *The Quarterly Journal of the Library of Congress* 27 (27 October 1970), 291–94.

Bejach, Lois D. "The Journal of a Civil War 'Commando'—DeWitt Clinton Fort." *The West Tennessee Historical Society Papers.* Vol. 11 (1948), 5–32.

Bodnia, George. "Fort Pillow 'Massacre'—Observations of a Minnesotan." *Minnesota Historical Society Collections* 43 (Spring 1973), 186–90.

Brewer, Theodore F. "Storming of Fort Pillow," *Confederate Veteran* 23 (December 1925), 459, 478.

Brobst, John F. *Civil War Letters of a Wisconsin Volunteer.* Madison: University of Wisconsin Press, 1960.

Castel, Albert. "The Fort Pillow Massacre: A Fresh Examination of the Evidence." *Civil War History* 4 (1958), 37–50.

———. "Fort Pillow Victory or Massacre." *American History Illustrated* 9 (April 1974), 4–10, 46–48.

Catton, Bruce. *The Army of the Potomac: Mr. Lincoln's Army.* Vol. 1. New York: Doubleday and Company, 1951, 1962.

———. *Never Call Retreat.* New York: Doubleday and Company, Inc., 1965.

Chalmers, James R. "Nathan Bedford Forrest and His Campaigns." *Southern Historical Society Papers* 7 (August 1879), 451–72.

Cimprich, John, and Robert C. Mainfort, Jr. "Fort Pillow Revisited: New Evidence About an Old Controversy," *Civil War History* 28 (December 1982), 293–306.

———. "Dr. Fitch's Report on the Fort Pillow Massacre." *Tennessee Historical Quarterly* 44 (Spring 1985), 27–39.

———. "Fort Pillow Massacre: A Statistical Note," *Journal of American History* 76 (December 1989), 830–37.

Clark, Achilles V. "A Letter of Account: Sergeant Clark Tells of the Fort Pillow Massacre." Edited by Dan E. Pomeroy. *Civil War Times Illustrated* 24 (June 1985).

Cornish, Dudley Taylor. *The Sable Arm: Black Troops in the Union Army, 1861–1865.* Lawrence: University Press of Kansas, 1987.

Cummings, Kate. "Our Evacuation of Fort Pillow (A letter from Edwin H. Sessel)." *Confederate Veteran* 6 (January 1893), 32–33.

Dinkins, James. "The Capture of Fort Pillow." *Confederate Veteran* 23 (December 1925), 460–62.

Fitch, Charles. "Letter to General Chalmers (May 13, 1879)." *Southern Historical Society Papers* 7 (13 August 1879), 440–41.

Foote, Shelby. *Red River to Appomatox.* New York: Random House, 1974.

"Forrest, Nathan Bedford." *Civil War Times.* Jamestown, Va.: Eastern National Park and Monument Association, Eastern Acorn Press, 1988.

Gallagher, Gary W., ed. *Fighting for the Confederacy: The Personal Recollections of General Edward Porter Alexander.* Chapel Hill: University of North Carolina Press, 1989.

Glatthaar, Joseph T. *Forged in Battle, The Civil War Alliance of Black Soldiers and White Officers.* New York: Free Press, 1990.

Grant, Ulysses S. *Memoirs and Selected Letters, Personal Memoirs of U. S. Grant, Selected Letters 1839–1865.* New York: The Library of America, 1990.

Hearn, Lafcadio. *Occidental Gleanings.* Edited by Albert Mordell. New York: Dodd Mead and Company, 1925.

Henry, Robert Selph. *Nathan Bedford Forrest: First with the Most.* New York: Mallard Press, 1991.

Huch, Ronald K. "The Fort Pillow Massacre: The Aftermath of Paducah." *Journal of the Illinois State Historical Society* 66 (Spring 1973), 62–70.

Hurst, Jack. *Nathan Bedford Forrest.* New York: Alfred A. Knopf, 1993.

Jordan, John L. "Was There a Massacre at Fort Pillow?" *Tennessee Historical Quarterly* 6 (June 1947), 99–133.

Jordan, General Thomas, and John P. Pryor. *The Campaigns of Lieut.-Gen. N. B. Forrest and of Forrest's Cavalry.* Dayton, Ohio: Morningside Bookshop, 1988.

McPherson, James M. *The Negro's Civil War.* New York: Pantheon Books, 1965.

———. *Battle Cry of Freedom, The Civil War Era.* New York: Ballantine Books, 1988.

Mainfort, Jr., Robert C. *Archaeological Investigations at Fort Pillow State Historical Area: 1976–1978.* Nashville: Division of Archaeology, Tennessee Department of Conservation, 1980.

Mays, Joe H. *Black Americans and Their Contribution toward Union Victory in the American Civil War 1861–1865.* Lanham, Md.: University Press of America, 1984.

Memphis Argus, issue of 14 April 1864.

Memphis Bulletins, issues of 15, 16, and 17 April 1864.

Miller, Francis T., ed. *The Photographic History of the Civil War.* 10 vols. New York: Review of Reviews Co., 1911.

Mitchell, Reid. *Civil War Soldiers, Their Expectations and Their Experiences.* New York: Viking Penguin, 1988.

New York Evening Post, issues between 15 April 1864 and 4 May 1864.

New York Herald, issues between 14 April 1864 and 4 May 1864.

New York Times, issues between 14 April 1864 and 4 May 1864.

Nicolay, John J., and John Hay. *Complete Works of Abraham Lincoln.* Vol. 10. Cumberland Gap, Tenn.: Lincoln Memorial University, 1894.

Quarles, Benjamin. *The Negro in the Civil War.* New York: Russell and Russell, 1987.

Sandburg, Carl. *Abraham Lincoln, The War Years.* Vol. 3. New York: Harcourt, Brace and World, 1939.

Sheppard, William Eric. *Bedford Forrest, The Confederacy's Greatest Cavalryman.* Dayton, Ohio: Morningside House, Inc. 1988.

Sherman, William Tecumseh. *Memoirs of General W. T. Sherman.* New York: Library of America, 1990.

Strong, Robert Hale. *A Yankee Private's Civil War.* Edited by Ashley Halsey. Chicago: Henry Regney Company, 1961.

U. S. Government. House Reports, No. 65, 38th Cong., 1st Sess., Joint Committee on the Conduct of the War, *Fort Pillow Massacre.* Washington, D.C.: 1864.

———. Government Report of the Joint Select Committee to Inquire into the Condition of Affairs in the Late Insurrectionary States. *Klu Klux Conspiracy,* 42 Cong., 2d Sess., Senate Report No. 41, Vol. 13. Washington, D.C.: 1872.

———. *War of the Rebellion, A Compilation of the Official Records of the Union and Confederate Armies,* 128 vols. Washington, D.C.: U.S. Government Printing Office, 1880–1901.

———. *War of the Rebellion: Official Records of the Union and the Confederate Navies,* 31 Vols. Washington, D.C.: U.S. Government Printing Office, 1894–1927.

Williams, George W. *A History of the Negro Troops in the War of the Rebellion.* New York: Negro Universities Press, 1969.

Wills, Brian Steel. *A Battle from the Start.* New York: Harper-Collins, 1992.

Wyeth, John A. "The Storming of Fort Pillow," *Harpers New Monthly Magazine* 99, no. 592 (September 1869), 595–607.

Wyeth, John A. *The Life of General Nathan Bedford Forrest.* New York: Harper and Brothers, 1899. Reprint. *That Devil Forrest: The Life of General Nathan Bedford Forrest.* New York: Harper and Brothers, 1959.

Young, Bennett H. *Confederate Wizards of the Saddle.* Dayton, Ohio: Morningside House, Inc, 1988.

Index